Stand True to the Charge

Stand True to the Charge

An Exposition of I Timothy

ROBERT G. GROMACKI

BAKER BOOK HOUSE
Grand Rapids, Michigan 49506

ISBN: 0-8010-3786-7

PHOTOLITHOPRINTED BY CUSHING - MALLOY, INC.
ANN ARBOR, MICHIGAN, UNITED STATES OF AMERICA

To
these Christian women
whose good works have been
a blessing to my family and me

Mary Armstrong
Helen Eisenhart
Miriam Maddox
Bernice Mick
Inez Milner
Lena Yoder

1

Contents

Preface

Someone has said that the greatest ability is dependability. The basic requirement of a steward is faithfulness. In all areas of life, employers and leaders are looking for people whom they can trust, people who will be loyal, people who can be counted on to perform assigned tasks.

These qualities are especially needed in Christian leaders. In this epistle, Paul gave directives to Timothy, who was to minister in Ephesus as the apostle's designated representative. These charges set forth principles for the dependable, faithful servant of God. They also contain guidelines for the life of the local church. A study of this epistle, therefore, will prove helpful for both the pastor and his congregation.

This study has been designed to teach the Word of God to others. It is an attempt to make clear the meaning of the English text (King James Version) through organization, exposition, and careful use of the Greek text. It is planned as a readable study, using a nontechnical vocabulary and smooth transitions from one section to the next. The words of the English text are in quotation marks for easy reference, the Greek words are transliterated, and necessary grammatical explanations have been put into the footnotes. This study also contains a wealth of cross-references to other supporting passages of Scripture.

Divided into thirteen chapters, this book can be used by adult Sunday-school classes or Bible-study groups for a traditional quarter of thirteen weeks. Concluding each chapter are discussion questions, designed to stimulate personal inquiry and to make the truth of

God relevant. This book can also be used as a private Bible-study guide by both the pastor and the layman. In all situations, however, this book should be read with an open Bible in front of the student. It is my prayer that men and women will be blessed and edified as they undertake this study of I Timothy.

This volume will complement my other expositions: *Called to Be Saints* (I Corinthians); *Stand Firm in the Faith* (II Corinthians); *Stand Fast in Liberty* (Galatians); *Stand United in Joy* (Philippians); and *Stand Perfect in Wisdom* (Colossians and Philemon).

A special word of thanks is extended to Cornelius Zylstra and Dan Van't Kerkhoff, editors at Baker Book House, who encouraged and assisted me in this project.

Also, my love and appreciation go to my dear wife, Gloria, who carefully typed the manuscript.

Introduction

I. AUTHORSHIP OF THE PASTORAL EPISTLES

The books of I Timothy, II Timothy, and Titus have been called the pastoral Epistles because in them Paul gave instructions to his young associates about the spiritual oversight or pastoral care of their respective churches. Timothy and Titus were not pastors per se; rather, they were apostolic representatives sent to Ephesus and Crete respectively to supervise the proper organization and function of the churches under the leadership of trained pastors and deacons. In the personal charges given to them, however, are principles applicable to local church leaders of all generations.

Of all the thirteen Pauline Epistles, the authorship of these three has been questioned most severely by modern critics. This has been done in spite of the strong testimony of the church fathers. These accepted the books as canonical and written by Paul: Ignatius, Polycarp, Justin Martyr, Clement of Alexandria, Tertullian, and Irenaeus. The pastoral Epistles were also listed in the Pauline section of the Muratorian canon. The Fathers' decisions reflect the internal witness of the books. All three books begin with the claim that the writer was Paul the apostle (I Tim. 1:1; cf. 2:7; II Tim. 1:1; Titus 1:1). The author's analysis of his spiritual past (I Tim. 1:11-15) agrees with the account in the Book of Acts. His identification of Timothy and Titus as his "sons" in the faith is definitely a Pauline designation (I Tim. 1:2, 18; II Tim. 1:2; 2:1; Titus 1:4).

Some scholars who have rejected Pauline authorship view the Pastorals as pseudonymous[1] writings, written either by a second-

1. The word *pseudonym* is derived from a Greek word that means "falsely

century opponent of Gnosticism or by a follower of Paul who (after the apostle's martyrdom) incorporated some genuine Pauline material into pseudonymous letters.[2] However, this conclusion is highly subjective. Who determines what is authentic? Why are most of the genuine passages found in II Timothy? Why did the pseudonymous writer compose three books? Could he not have achieved his purpose by writing merely one? Would not the writing of three pseudonymous books be more suspect than the writing of one? Actually, pseudonymous writings were rejected by the early church, not accepted. Although such a practice may have been acceptable in the pagan world, it did not meet the standard of honesty and authenticity required of canonical books. Paul warned against such forgeries carrying his name (II Thess. 2:2–3). Authorship by an apostle or by an authoritative associate of an apostle was deemed necessary as the basis of acceptance by the church.

The arguments set forth against Pauline authorship are many. First, the rejection of these books by some second-century church fathers (Basilides, Tatian, and Marcion) has caused some people to doubt. However, these men were Gnostic heretics who disagreed with some of the content of these letters. When Paul stated that the law was good (I Tim. 1:8) and that Timothy should avoid "profane and vain babblings, and oppositions of science falsely so called" (I Tim. 6:20), he mentioned concepts contrary to the philosophy of Marcion.[3] It is no wonder that these three men rejected the epistles.

Second, critics believe that there are some discrepancies between the historical data in the Pastorals and those recorded in Acts and found in the recognized Pauline writings. However, this charge is based upon the assumption that Paul was imprisoned only once in Rome. Paul's release from his first internment at Rome, a subsequent ministry for two or three years, and a second imprisonment at Rome

---

named." This does not refer to an author writing under a pen name (e.g., Samuel Clemens writing as Mark Twain). Rather it refers to a writer who uses the name of a real person, living or dead. This writer may firmly believe that he has written what the other person would have penned had the latter been around to do so.

2. These passages have been suggested as being authentic: I Timothy 1:13–15; II Timothy 1:4–5, 16–18; 3:10–15; 4:1–2a, 5b–22; Titus 3:12–15.

3. The phrase "oppositions of science falsely so called" is based upon the Greek *antitheseis tēs pseudōnumou gnōseōs*. Note the use of "antithesis" and "gnosis," terms emphasized by Marcion.

can easily account for the difference in historical data. Paul did expect to be released from his first imprisonment (Phil. 1:25; Philem. 22) and he apparently was released. Some church fathers (Clement of Rome, Eusebius) mentioned a Pauline ministry in the west, possibly Spain (cf. Rom. 15:24). This could have been accomplished in the interval between the two imprisonments. The Pastorals describe the movements of Paul after the history of Acts was recorded (A.D. 30–61; cf. A.D. 61–64). In these closing years Paul visited Ephesus (I Tim. 1:3), Crete (Titus 1:5), Nicopolis (Titus 3:12), Corinth (II Tim. 4:20), Miletus (II Tim. 4:20), and Troas (II Tim. 4:13), and was finally taken to Rome (II Tim. 1:17).

Third, some scholars have claimed that the organization of local churches that is described in the Pastorals is too advanced for the actual time of Paul's ministry. However, the appointment and the assigned responsibilities of the bishop-pastor-elder were an integral part of Paul's ministry of edification (Acts 14:23; 15:2–6; 20:17–28) and of Peter's admonitions (I Peter 5:1–4). The concept of the function of the deacon developed very early in the church (Acts 6:1–6; cf. Phil. 1:1). Women always played an important role in church life (Acts 9:36–39; 16:14–15; Rom. 16:1). The care of a designated group of widows prompted the creation of the diaconate (Acts 6:1–6). Proper order within worship services had developed before the writing of the Pastorals (I Cor. 11–14).

Fourth, critics believe that the false teaching attacked in the Pastorals is the Gnostic heresy of the second century. They point out that celibacy and a vegetarian diet (I Tim. 4:3) were common characteristics of advanced Gnosticism. However, the heresy discussed in the Pastorals still had a strong Jewish influence (I Tim. 1:3–10; Titus 1:10, 14; 3:9). This corresponds more to the incipient Judaistic Gnosticism refuted in Colossians than to the mature philosophical Gnosticism of the second century.

The fifth argument is that the style, vocabulary, and doctrinal outlook in the Pastorals are radically different from that in the other Pauline Epistles. It is a fact that there are 175 words in the Pastorals that are not found elsewhere in the New Testament.[4] However, the

4. These words are called *hapax legomena,* "words spoken only once."

difference in subject matter would account for most of this. A man's style normally changes with increasing age and experience. Actually this is an indirect argument for Pauline authorship. Would a forger have incorporated so many unique words if he were trying to pass off the books as Pauline originals? Would he have dared to call the beloved apostle Paul the "chief" of sinners?

The arguments advanced against the Pauline authorship of the Pastorals are not as strong as they initially appear to be. Evangelical answers are readily available. Until better evidence is forthcoming, it must be concluded that both the external and the internal evidence support the Pauline authorship of these books.

II. LIFE OF TIMOTHY

A native of Lystra, Timothy was the son of a Greek father and a Jewish mother (Acts 16:1). In his early youth he was influenced by the godly lives of his grandmother Lois and his mother Eunice (II Tim. 1:5; 3:15). He apparently was converted to Christ by Paul during the latter's first missionary journey (I Tim. 1:2, 18; cf. Acts 14:6–23).[5] Because of Timothy's spiritual gifts and rapid maturation as a Christian, Paul selected him during the second journey to become an associate in the missionary enterprise (Acts 16:1–3). At that time he was circumcised[6] and ordained (Acts 16:3; I Tim. 4:14; II Tim. 4:5).

Timothy shared in the establishment of the works at Philippi, Thessalonica, and Berea (Acts 16:1—17:14). When he rejoined Paul at Athens, he was sent back to Thessalonica to continue the edification of that church (Acts 17:14–16; cf. I Thess. 3:1–2). He later returned to Paul at Corinth and assisted the apostle in the founding of that church (Acts 18:5). The biblical record is silent as to whether Timothy traveled with Paul from Corinth to Ephesus to Caesarea to Jerusalem to Antioch and finally back to Ephesus (Acts 18:18—19:1).

5. Paul's constant mention of Timothy as his son doubtless refers to the latter's conversion as well as the close relationship that developed between them.

6. The circumcision of Timothy was not a contradiction of Paul's teaching (cf. Gal. 5:2–3). He was circumcised not to gain justification but to increase his effectiveness as a witness to Jewish audiences who knew his ethnic background (cf. I Cor. 9:19–20).

However, he did work with Paul at Ephesus (Acts 19:22). Paul then sent him into the provinces of Macedonia and Achaia to minister to the churches in those areas and to prepare the way for a proposed visit by Paul (Acts 19:22; cf. I Cor. 4:17; 16:10). Before Paul left Ephesus, Timothy rejoined him in that city (Rom. 16:21; II Cor. 1:1, 19).[7] He then traveled with Paul from Ephesus to Macedonia to Achaia, back to Macedonia, and on to the province of Asia (Acts 20:1-5). Again, the biblical record is silent about the presence of Timothy on Paul's trip to Jerusalem, his arrest at the holy city, his two-year imprisonment at Caesarea, and his voyage to Rome (Acts 21:1—28:16). However, since Timothy was with Paul at Rome (Phil. 1:1; 2:19; Col. 1:1; Philem. 1), he probably also was with Paul during those years. If he was not, then he must have rejoined Paul at Rome in the early months of the apostle's imprisonment. From Rome he may have been sent to Philippi (Phil. 2:19-24), although Paul's release may have prevented that desire from being fulfilled. After Paul's release, Timothy journeyed with the apostle to Ephesus, where he was left to care for the church (I Tim. 1:3). He was not with Paul when the latter was arrested and quickly taken to Rome. However, Paul requested that he come to Rome (II Tim. 4:9). It is difficult to say whether Timothy did go to Rome and whether he arrived before the apostle's martyrdom. If Paul wrote Hebrews,[8] there is some speculation that Timothy went to Rome, was imprisoned, and was later released (Heb. 13:23-24). Tradition states that Timothy was martyred during the reign of either Domitian or Nerva.

III. TIME AND PLACE

After Paul was acquitted by the emperor and released from his first Roman imprisonment (A.D. 61), he resumed his missionary activities and was accompanied by Timothy, Titus, Luke, and possibly some others. Contrary to what he had earlier thought, Paul

7. Timothy was gone when Paul wrote I Corinthians, but he was with the apostle when II Corinthians was written. Note the respective omission and inclusion of his name in the salutations.

8. The speculation could stand even if Hebrews were written by one other than Paul after the apostle's martyrdom.

was able to return to Ephesus; there he left Timothy in charge while he moved on to Macedonia (I Tim. 1:3; cf. Acts 20:25, 37-38). Paul expected to rejoin Timothy at Ephesus but he was not sure about the time of his arrival (I Tim. 3:14; 4:13). Thinking that he might be delayed longer than he had expected, Paul thus wrote to Timothy to encourage and instruct him in his many tasks: "But if I tarry long, that thou mayest know how thou oughtest to behave thyself in the house of God, which is the church of the living God, the pillar and ground of the truth" (3:15). The book therefore was written from Macedonia about A.D. 62, although some scholars have suggested either A.D. 63 or 64.

IV. PURPOSES

Because Paul's approach was very methodical, his purposes in writing are clear. He wanted to charge Timothy to oppose the false, legalistic teachers (1), to outline the nature and purposes of prayer in the public worship service (2:1-8), to discuss the spiritual responsibilities of women (2:9-15), to list the qualifications of the bishop-pastor-elder (3:1-7) and of the deacons (3:8-13), to explain his plans for rejoining Timothy (3:14-16), and to give guidance to Timothy about the latter's personal conduct (4:1—6:21). In these last three chapters Paul charged his young associate to warn the church about the future moral and doctrinal apostasy (4:1-6), to develop spiritual maturity for his own benefit and that of his congregation (4:7-16), to provide financial care for the elderly Christian widows within the church (5:1-16), to exercise wisdom in the ordination, support, and discipline of elders (5:17-25), to counsel the Christian slaves about their relationships with their masters (6:1-2), to withdraw himself from false, greedy teachers (6:3-10), to avoid these errors and to develop a positive Christian life (6:11-16), to admonish the wealthy believers to be good stewards of God's money (6:17-20), and to avoid philosophical speculation (6:20-21).

1

The Opening Charge
I Timothy 1:1–11

The personal relationship between Paul and Timothy was warm and intimate. Ever since Timothy joined the apostle on the second journey (Acts 16:1–3), Paul viewed his younger associate as his son. Other believers were aware of this special rapport: "But ye know the proof of [Timothy], that, as a son with the father, he hath served with me in the gospel" (Phil. 2:22). Paul and Timothy were "like-minded" in their selfless, loving concern for the churches (Phil. 2:20–21). Usually they traveled together, but occasionally Paul sent Timothy on assigned tasks (I Cor. 4:17; Phil. 2:19; I Thess. 3:2). Timothy's faithfulness and efficiency must have caused the apostle to place great confidence in him.

In this epistle, the aged missionary-evangelist entrusted another responsibility to his beloved companion. The book begins and ends with the commands of the spiritual general to his subordinate officer (1:3; 6:14, 17, 20). Paul fully expected that his trustworthy friend would execute his orders.

I. THE SALUTATION (1:1–2)

These introductory remarks contain some of the distinctive features of a Pauline epistle: Paul's name and description, the identity of his reader, and a spiritual greeting.

A. Author (1:1)

1. His name

Born into the Jewish tribe of Benjamin, Paul was probably named by his parents after the first king of Israel, Saul (Phil. 3:5; cf. I Sam. 9:1–2). In Paul's pre-Christian life, he was known as Saul of Tarsus, the persecutor of the church (Acts 7:58; 8:1, 3; 9:1). When Christ revealed Himself to the young Pharisee, He addressed him as Saul (Acts 9:4). For the next nine years of Paul's Christian life, he used that given name (Acts 9:17, 19, 22, 26; 11:25, 30; 13:1–2).

Since persons born in bilingual countries were often given two names, some scholars have conjectured that the apostle also received the name *Paul* (*Paulos*) at birth.[1] The apostle did come from a Jewish family that possessed Roman citizenship and lived in Tarsus, the chief city of Cilicia and one of the great learning centers of the Eastern world.

A more plausible explanation is that the apostle changed his name from Saul to Paul at the beginning of his first missionary journey (Acts 13:9, 13). On this occasion, at Cyprus, he demonstrated his apostolic authority for the first time by imposing blindness upon the sorcerer Elymas, who had resisted the gospel witness. Through this miracle, he won his first convert, the Roman proconsul Sergius Paulus (Acts 13:7–12). It is reasonable to conclude that Paul assumed this man's name as a constant reminder of the grace and power of God, who can save sinners and call them into Christian service.[2] Otherwise, it would have been a mere coincidence that Luke recorded the change in the apostle's name in the midst of this narrative detailing the salvation experience of the Roman deputy.

The Latin word *paulus* means "little" or "small." The English noun *pauper* is derived from it. In a true spiritual analogy, Paul saw himself as "the least of all saints" (Eph. 3:8) and as the "chief" of sinners (1:15). This new name manifested the change from the pride of Phariseeism to the humility of Christianity. Before God,

1. D. Edmond Hiebert, *First Timothy* (Chicago: Moody, 1957), p. 19.

2. Two early church fathers, Jerome and Augustine, both believed that Paul took his new name from Sergius Paulus.

Paul was conscious of his smallness. He may have been small in stature (II Cor. 10:1, 10). A man is known by his name, and Paul epitomized his.

2. *His position*

Why did Paul identify himself as an apostle when he wrote to his loyal associate, his son in the faith? Paul assigned Timothy several tasks at Ephesus. The church needed to know that Timothy, as Paul's designated representative, had the authority to issue instructions and be sure the church followed those instructions.

Paul characterized his position in four ways. First, he claimed to be "an apostle" (*apostolos*). He employed this official title for himself several times (Rom. 1:1; I Cor. 1:1; II Cor. 1:1; Eph. 1:1; II Tim. 1:1; Titus 1:1). Apostles were those believers who had seen the resurrected Christ and who had been commanded directly by Him to preach and lay the foundation for the church age (Eph. 2:20).[3] Their ministries were authenticated by miracles (Mark 16:17, 20; Heb. 2:3–4). Paul thus qualified for this authoritative position (I Cor. 9:1; II Cor. 12:12). Actually, few men bore this title: the Twelve, Matthias (Acts 1:26), Barnabas (Acts 14:14), James the Lord's brother (Gal. 1:19), and Paul.[4]

Second, Paul was an apostle "of Jesus Christ." Christ both saved him and sent him forth (Acts 26:16; I Cor. 9:1; 15:8–10).[5] The others became apostles during the Lord's earthly and preascension ministries, but Paul received that office through a unique, postascension appearance. His apostleship nevertheless was recognized as genuine by the Jerusalem apostles (Gal. 2:1–10).

Third, Paul became an apostle by "commandment" (*epitagēn*). This military term literally means "upon order or rank." It is used seven times in the New Testament (Rom. 16:26; I Cor. 7:6, 25; II Cor.

3. The Greek word *apostolos,* translated "apostle," comes from the verb *apostellō,* which means "to send away with a commission to do something." The original twelve apostles were selected from among many disciples to be with Christ and to be sent forth by Him to preach, heal, and cast out demons within Israel (Matt. 10:5–8; Mark 3:13–15). Excluding Judas Iscariot, this group was later recommissioned by the resurrected Christ to preach the gospel throughout the world (Matt. 28:16–20).

4. It may be that Barnabas was an apostle in a nontechnical sense in that he was sent by the church at Antioch, but not directly by Christ (Acts 13:1–4).

5. The name "Jesus Christ" thus is seen as a subjective genitive.

8:8; I Tim. 1:1; Titus 1:3; 2:15). Its verb form is used of Christ commanding the unclean spirits to leave a human body (Mark 1:27; 9:25) and the winds to stop blowing (Luke 8:25). Other examples of this authoritative term are the command of Herod Antipas to decapitate John the Baptist (Mark 6:27) and the shout of the priest Ananias to smite Paul (Acts 23:2). The will of God issued in this direct command to Paul (Eph. 1:11; II Tim. 1:1). Paul recognized the necessity of total submission to such divine authority and thus confessed that he "was not disobedient unto the heavenly vision" (Acts 26:19).

Fourth, the commandment had a double source: the Father and the Son. The Father is identified as "God our Saviour." The term "Saviour" (*sōtēros*) is used ten times in the Pastorals: six times for the Father (I Tim. 1:1; 2:3; 4:10; Titus 1:3; 2:10; 3:4) and four times for the Son (II Tim. 1:10; Titus 1:4; 2:13; 3:6). The Father is the ultimate source of salvation, whereas the Son is the channel. The pagans considered Zeus their savior; emperor worship began when Nero wanted to be revered as the empire's savior-god. God, however, declared concerning Himself, ". . . there is no God else beside me; a just God and a Saviour; there is none beside me" (Isa. 45:21). The Savior must be divine, and only God can save. Salvation rests in the divine Being, not in a program or in self. The Son, the Lord Jesus Christ, is depicted as "our hope." He is the substance and foundation of our spiritual optimism. He not only gives hope, but He also *is* hope. Elsewhere, Christ is called "the hope of glory" (Col. 1:27) and "that blessed hope" (Titus 2:13). Biblical hope denotes absolute certainty of fulfillment. From the apostle's perspective, the concept of salvation looked back to the past, whereas the quality of hope viewed the future. Timothy needed this double reminder as he contemplated his awesome responsibilities in Ephesus.

B. Recipient (1:2)

1. His name

Timothy's name was based upon two words: "honor" (*timaō*) and "God" (*theos*).[6] He was one who honored God and one whom

6. Consult the material about the life of Timothy in the introduction.

God honored (I Sam. 2:30). His name occurs seventeen times in ten different Pauline epistles, more often than that of any other companion of the apostle.

2. His position

Paul identified Timothy as his "own son in the faith." The word "own" (*gnēsiōi*) literally means "nothing spurious," "genuine," "lawfully begotten." It is used elsewhere of Titus (Titus 1:4) and of an anonymous yokefellow (Phil. 4:3).

Timothy was a spiritual, not biological, son of Paul. The prepositional phrase actually reads "in faith" (*en pistei*). The absence of the definite article points to the quality of faith necessary for salvation and the daily walk, not to the body of doctrinal truth embraced by all believers.

C. Greeting (1:2)

1. Nature of the greeting

Three blessings are requested for Timothy. First, the essence of "grace" (*charis*) emphasizes the constant outpouring of divine favor upon undeserving men (John 1:16). The justified position of the redeemed sinner is both based upon and maintained by divine grace (Rom. 3:24; Eph. 2:8–9). In addition, God supplies daily grace for present needs.

Second, the concept of "mercy" (*eleos*) stresses divine compassion and pity. The psalmist declared, "Like as a father pitieth his children, so the LORD pitieth them that fear him. For he knoweth our frame; he remembereth that we are dust" (Ps. 103:13–14). Believers crave mercy when they need forgiveness, encouragement, and support.

Third, the term "peace" points to the peace *of* God for daily protection from hostile pressures upon a believer's mind and heart (Phil. 4:7). This type of peace is based upon judicial peace *with* God, which is gained at regeneration (Rom. 5:1).

2. Source of blessing

The source of this blessing is two persons within the divine Being. The single preposition "from" (*apo*) links the Father and the Son as the common source.[7] Doubtless these gifts are mediated to the believer through the indwelling ministry of the Holy Spirit.

II. THE CHARGE (1:3-11)

The concept of charge is dominant in this epistle. The verb (*paraggellō*) is used five times (1:3; 4:11; 5:7; 6:13, 17) and its noun form is found twice (1:5, 18). The term suggests the transfer of commands from a superior officer to a subordinate. Paul fully expected that Timothy, as a "good soldier of Jesus Christ" (II Tim. 2:3), would carry out the apostolic charge.

A. The Charge and Legalism (1:3-7)

The geographical movements of Paul after his release from his first Roman imprisonment are difficult to trace. He apparently went to the island of Crete, where he left Titus in charge of the work (Titus 1:5). He expected to visit Philemon in Colosse (Philem. 22). If Timothy left the apostle before Paul's release, then the young associate must have rejoined Paul in Ephesus after a brief stop in Philippi (Phil. 2:23). At Ephesus, then, their paths crisscrossed again (1:3). Since Paul had planned to visit the Philippians (Phil. 2:24), he left Timothy and traveled into Macedonia.

Since Paul "besought [Timothy] to abide" (1:3) in that Asian city, there may have been some reluctance on Timothy's part to stay there. The oppressive nature of the unbelieving Ephesians and the natural timidity of Timothy caused Paul to issue such a command to his spiritual son (cf. Acts 19:23-41; I Cor. 16:8-9).

7. The deity of Jesus Christ is affirmed in this verse by the divine title "Lord" and by His union with the Father as the common source of grace, mercy, and peace.

1. Purposes of the charge (1:3–4)

Two purposes are indicated by the conjunction "that" (*hina*). Timothy, with the full force of delegated apostolic authority invested in him, charged "some" (*tisi*) within the assembly, but not all. The use of this indefinite pronoun shows that the problem of false teaching was to be solved on the basis of principle rather than personality. No proper names are given, unless Hymenaeus and Alexander were two of the heretical teachers (1:20).

The first purpose dealt with public proclamation of error. Timothy was to charge some "that they teach no other doctrine" (*mē heterodidaskalein*). The false teachers were to stop doing what they had been doing.[8] This compound verb form contains the adjective "other" (*heteros*), which connotes "another of a different kind." Elsewhere, Paul warned against receiving "another [*heteron*] spirit, which ye have not received, or another [*heteron*] gospel, which ye have not accepted" (II Cor. 11:4). He also cautioned the Galatians not to move from "the grace of Christ unto another [*heteron*] gospel: which is not another" (*allo;* Gal. 1:6–7).[9] The difference was not in the manner of preaching, but in the content of the message. The legalists promoted doctrinal error, not truth. Such teaching is deceptive and damnable; thus, the curse of God will fall upon its proponents (Gal. 1:8–9). Paul's earlier prediction, given to the Ephesian elders, had sadly come to pass: "For I know this, that after my departing shall grievous wolves enter in among you, not sparing the flock. Also of your own selves shall men arise, speaking perverse things, to draw away disciples after them" (Acts 20:29–30).

The second purpose was concerned with the willful, mental acceptance of error. Paul charged the same group not to "give heed to fables and endless genealogies." The verb form "give heed" (*prosechein*) means "to attach oneself to, to adhere to, to hold to, to give assent to." It involves an active, constant commitment to a cause.[10]

8. Indicated by the present active infinitive with the negative. The term *heterodoxy* is based upon this verb.

9. For example, a boy, who ate some fruit (McIntosh apple), was given another or different (*heteron*) fruit (Bartlett pear), which was not another (Delicious apple; *allo*).

10. The verb form is a present active infinitive.

Such wrong commitment had two objects: "fables and endless genealogies." The first term, "fables" (*muthois*), transliterates into English as "myths."[11] When a person is sound in the faith, he will not give heed "to Jewish fables, and commandments of men, that turn from the truth" (Titus 1:14). The problem, which both Timothy and Titus encountered, was the error of the Judaizers who insisted that circumcision and obedience to the Mosaic law were necessary for both justification and sanctification (Acts 15:1). The Judaizers' myths probably involved clever, logical deductions from the events surrounding Old Testament men of faith. Their conclusions, however, were faulty because they were based upon the wrong principle of legalism.

The second phrase, "endless genealogies," may refer either to the allegorizing of Old Testament lists of names or to the study of Jewish genealogical registers. The Judaizers may have tried to impress the Gentile converts with their lineage. Some scholars have suggested that the genealogies deal with the angelic emanations that the Judaistic, Gnostic heretics elevated as the means of creation (Col. 2:18). Regardless, such mental musings were "endless" (*aperantois*) in that they were useless and of no practical spiritual value. No relevant conclusions about the problems of life could be drawn from them.

Paul then pointed out that such faulty reasonings only "minister questions." The Judaizers had questions, but no answers. The term "questions" (*zētēseis*) refers to investigations, toilsome inquiry, and inconclusive disputations.

Proper teaching will issue in "godly edifying" (*oikodomian theou*).[12] Only God is the source of regeneration and edification, and these are accomplished through truth and love (Eph. 4:14–16). This edification operates "in faith" (*en pistei*). The absence of the definite article *the* indicates that the body of doctrinal truth essential to the evangelical faith is not being considered here. Rather, men are justified by faith and they must subsequently walk by faith (Rom. 1:17). Obedience to the law has no part in justification or sanctification.

11. The word occurs five times in the New Testament: I Timothy 1:4; 4:7; II Timothy 4:4; Titus 1:14; II Peter 1:16.

12. The critical text reads "dispensation" (*oikonomian*).

2. Goal of the charge (1:5)

Up to this point, the charge has been negative in character (1:3–4). In this verse, the apostle stressed the positive goal of the admonition: "charity" (*agapē*). The term "end" (*telos*) looks at the goal or purpose of achievement, which takes time.[13] The influence of the false teachers led to mental fascination and legal conformity, but the acceptance of the apostolic directive effected love for God, for the family of God, and for the truth of God.

Although the law taught that men should love their neighbors as themselves, it did not supply the inner dynamic to do so. Such love "is shed abroad in our hearts by the Holy Ghost which is given unto us" (Rom. 5:5). The term "commandment" (*paraggelias*) does not refer to any one or all of the Ten Commandments; rather, it refers to the verb "charge" (*paraggeilēis;* 1:3). This Greek term is not used in the New Testament as a synonym for the Mosaic law.

Such genuine love does not have its source ("out of"; *ek*) in self or in legalism. Christ commanded His own to love each other as He had loved them (John 13:34–35). He changed the standard of love from horizontal and human to vertical and divine. According to Paul, this type of love comes from a triple source. First, this love can only emerge from "a pure heart" (*katharas kardias*). A pure heart is literally a "cleansed" heart. A person who has experienced the divine washing of regeneration is regarded as clean before God (John 13:10–11; I Cor. 6:11; Titus 3:5). Regeneration is accomplished by the blood of Christ, by the Word of God, and by the ministry of the Holy Spirit (John 15:3; Rev. 1:5). In the Sermon on the Mount, Jesus declared, "Blessed are the pure in heart: for they shall see God" (Matt. 5:8). The biblical term *heart* points to the center of human life. Donald Guthrie notes, ". . . and without purity there, nobility of character is clearly impossible."[14]

Second, this love stems from a "good conscience" (*suneidēseōs agathēs*). Made in the image of God, man is a moral personality. He has an innate sense of what he ought to do, an intuitive concept of right and wrong. Conscience causes the inner self to sit in moral

13. The word *telescope* contains this Greek term.

14. *The Pastoral Epistles,* Tyndale Bible Commentary (Grand Rapids: Eerdmans, 1972), p. 59.

judgment upon its attitudes and actions. Warren W. Wiersbe observes, "Conscience is the inner judge that accuses us when we have done wrong and approves when we have done right."[15] In his sinful state, man excuses or justifies his wrongdoing (Rom. 2:15). Many sinners develop seared consciences (4:2). A "good" conscience is one that measures itself by the moral goodness of God who alone is good in Himself (Mark 10:18).

Third, this love originates from a "faith unfeigned." It is literally an "unhypocritical" (*anupokritou*) faith. The term *hupokritēs* was used in ancient Greece of an actor on stage who pretended to be what he was not. Genuine faith needs no masquerade; it is open for all men to see. In it, belief and behavior correspond.

3. Perversion of the charge (1:6-7)

A fourfold description of the false teachers who were the objects of the apostolic charge is now given. First, they "swerved" (*astochēsantes*) from the positive moral virtues enumerated in the preceding verse: a pure heart, a good conscience, and an unhypocritical faith ("from which;" *hōn*).[16] The meaning of the verb is "to miss the mark." In legalistic attempts to gain a justified position before God, sinful man falls short. Paul ended this book in the same way that he began—with a ringing indictment against the egotistical attempts of self-righteous men: "which some professing have erred [*ēstochēsan*] concerning the faith" (6:21). In II Timothy, he criticized Hymenaeus and Philetus, "who concerning the truth have erred [*ēstochēsan*], saying that the resurrection is past already" (II Tim. 2:18). Moral error thus is the logical result of doctrinal error.

Second, these false teachers "turned aside unto vain jangling." This verb (*exetrapēsan*) is used five times in the New Testament (1:6; 5:15; 6:20; II Tim. 4:4; Heb. 12:13). It is a medical term that describes the dislocation of limbs. These teachers twisted doctrinal truths and turned people off course "unto vain jangling" (*eis mataiologian*). The phrase literally means "useless or aimless words" (cf. I Cor. 15:17). Such heresy can achieve no solid spiritual goals. Purposeless words can never satisfy the needy soul of man.

15. *Be Faithful* (Wheaton, IL: Victor Books, 1981), p. 59.
16. The relative pronoun "which" is plural.

Third, these teachers desired "to be teachers of the law" (*einai nomodidaskaloi*). The problem of legalism emerged shortly after Paul proclaimed the gospel to the pagan Roman and Greek world. The council at Jerusalem convened to discuss the issue of justification (Acts 15:1–20). That council recognized the heresy of legalism and acknowledged the harm it had caused: "Forasmuch as we have heard, that certain which went out from us have troubled you with words, subverting your souls, saying, Ye must be circumcised, and keep the law: to whom we gave no such commandment" (Acts 15:24). Paul identified these teachers as evil workers and enemies of the cross (Phil. 3:2, 18).[17]

Why does legalism permeate the religious world? Wiersbe notes, "The flesh (our old nature) loves religious legalism, because rules and regulations enable a person to appear holy without really having to change his heart."[18] The verb form "desiring" (*thelontes*) confirms that conclusion. By a constant choice of their own wills, men pursued that objective. They were thus morally culpable for their doctrinal deviation.

Fourth, the false teachers were ignorant ("understanding neither"). They had no perception in two areas. They did not understand what they said ("what they say"). They simply mouthed words, parroted what their teachers had impressively imposed upon them. They did not understand what they affirmed ("nor whereof they affirm"). The former statement dealt with the content of their teaching, whereas this second statement pointed to the emotional enthusiasm of their oratory. They were powerful in their preaching, but technique and excitement are not innate evidences of truth.

B. The Charge and the Law (1:8–11)

There is a difference between legalism and the law. To preach the law is not to preach legalism. In this section, Paul explained that distinction.

17. Hiebert, in *First Timothy,* p. 34, does not identify this group with the Judaizers.

18. *Be Faithful,* p. 18.

1. Use of the law (1:8–10)

Four assertions about the law are made. First, the law is "good" (*kalos*), not bad (cf. Rom. 7:16). Since God is good, He gives only that which is good, and the law came from Him through Moses (James 1:17). Elsewhere the apostle exclaimed, "Wherefore the law is holy, and the commandment holy, and just, and good" (*agathē;* Rom. 7:12). The law has both an intrinsic and an external goodness. It reveals the holiness of God and the sinfulness of man. Paul decried legalism, but he exalted the moral law of God codified in the Ten Commandments.

Second, the law has a proper use. How can a man "use it lawfully"? He must use the law as God intended it to be used; otherwise, he will abuse or misuse it. By the law is "the knowledge of sin" (Rom. 3:20). God has revealed His holy standards for attitude and behavior through the law. The breaking of those moral absolutes constitutes sin before a righteous God. Also, the law was given to create within man a consciousness of moral guilt and a confession of total inability to produce an ethical change within a person's life (Rom. 3:19). By the law, man must admit that he has sinned and that he is a guilty sinner deserving of eternal judgment. Finally, God planned that the law would drive men to God to be graciously justified by Him through faith in Christ (Gal. 3:24). In this sense, the law was a "schoolmaster" (Gal. 3:24).

Third, the law was not made "for a righteous man" (1:9a). The meaning of the word "law" (*nomos*) here is general; it goes beyond its specific revelation and application in the Mosaic law.[19] God never intended legalism, including the particular moral commandments in the law, to become the means of justification or sanctification. The reality of the spiritual life and the abundant life are not gained by compliance to a set of rules and regulations.

Fourth, the law was meant for the sinner (1:9b–10). It was designed to restrain evildoing and to punish the evildoer. Fourteen sinful groups are listed here.[20] The "lawless" (*anomois*) ignore law or

19. No definite article is used with *nomos;* compare 1:8 where the article is found.

20. The first eight constitute four sets of two names each, joined by the conjunction "and." The remaining six are mentioned individually. For other lists of sins, see Mark 7:20–23; Romans 1:18–32; Galatians 5:19–21.

refuse to recognize it. The "disobedient" literally are those "not under order" (*anupotaktois*). They are unruly and insubordinate. Kenneth S. Wuest remarks, "In the one case no legal obligation is *recognized;* in the other, subjection to law is *refused.*"[21]

The "ungodly" (*asebesi*) have no inner reverence for God. They willfully ignore Him. The "sinners" (*hamartōlois*) know what God has said, but they volitionally break or violate the law. They constantly fall short of God's glory (Rom. 3:23).

The "unholy" (*anosiois*) are devoid of piety or holiness. They are not devout. This is an indication of the last days (II Tim. 3:2). The "profane" (*bebēlois*) are thoroughly secularistic. This adjectival noun is based upon the Greek term for "threshold" (*bēlos*). These people metaphorically trample spiritual matters and treat them casually.

The "murderers of fathers" (*patralōiais*) and the "murderers of mothers" (*mētralōiais*) are rebellious children who mercilessly smite their parents. They violate the fifth commandment (Exod. 20:12).

The "manslayers" (*androphonois*) are actually killers of males, in violation of the sixth commandment (Exod. 20:13).[22]

The "whoremongers" (*pornois*) are harlots or fornicators. The word *pornography* is based upon this term. The phrase "them that defile themselves with mankind" (*arsenokoitais*) points to the sin of sodomy. The stress is on male homosexuality (I Cor. 6:9). The term literally reads "male coitus." Elsewhere, Paul described these people: "And likewise also the men [*arsenes*], leaving the natural use of the woman, burned in their lust one toward another: men with men working that which is unseemly . . ." (Rom. 1:27).

"The "menstealers" (*andrapodistais*) are those who buy and sell people as property. They are dealers in slaves. This could include the crime of kidnaping. The "liars" (*pseustais*) deliberately lie or bear false witness in violation of the ninth commandment (Exod. 20:16). The "perjured persons" (*epiorkois*) place lies upon (*epi*) an oath (*horkos*) to tell the truth. They violate both the third and ninth commandments (Exod. 20:7, 16).

21. *Word Studies in the Greek New Testament,* vol. 12, *The Pastoral Epistles* (Grand Rapids: Eerdmans, 1952), p. 31.

22. The prefix *andro* comes from *anēr,* used to indicate the husband or the male. The general word for "man" is *anthrōpos.*

This list is not exhaustive. In a generalization ("and if there be any other thing that is contrary to sound doctrine"), Paul argued that the law was designed for anyone who violated and opposed moral truth. Such obvious sins as idolatry and adultery are not mentioned here. The term "doctrine" (*didaskaliai*) can refer to both the act and the content of teaching. The word is used eight times in this book (1:10; 4:1, 6, 13, 16; 5:17; 6:1, 3). The nature of "sound" (*hugiainousēi*) doctrine is that it is spiritually and ethically wholesome and healthy. Such doctrine must also be accurate and truthful.

2. The law and the gospel (1:11)

Wiersbe observes,

> Law and Gospel go together, for the Law without the Gospel is diagnosis without remedy; but the Gospel without Law is only the Good News of salvation for people who don't believe they need it because they have never heard the bad news of judgment. The Law is not Gospel, but the Gospel is not lawless. . . .[23]

What is the standard of sound doctrine? The preposition "according to" (*kata*) introduces a threefold description of the divine norm. First, it is "the gospel" (*to euaggelion*). The word literally means "good message" or "good news." The content of the gospel centers in the person and redemptive work of Jesus Christ: His death for sins, burial, and physical resurrection (I Cor. 15:1–4).

Second, the standard is the gospel "of the glory of the blessed God" (*tēs doxēs tou makariou theou*).[24] The glory of God is outward manifestation of His essence. The gospel brings glory to God in that it displays His grace, love, mercy, and forgiveness. The adjective "blessed" is usually applied to the believer (Matt. 5:3), but it twice designates God (1:11; 6:15) and once refers to the hope of Christ's return (Titus 2:13).

Third, the gospel was committed into the trust of Paul. The verb (*episteuthēn*) looks back to the time when the apostle received his commission to preach from Christ.

23. *Be Faithful*, pp. 18–19.

24. The term is a noun ("glory") linked to God, rather than an adjective ("glorious") modifying the gospel. The same idea is found elsewhere (II Cor. 4:4).

Questions for Discussion

1. In what sense is God the Father our Savior? God the Son? Is this concept contradictory or complementary?
2. What is involved in having sons in the faith? How does the principle of discipleship fit into this plan?
3. How much time should be devoted to the public rebuke of doctrinal error from the pulpit? in the classroom? How can such truth be spoken in love?
4. What modern doctrinal controversies correspond to the myths Paul attacked? What types of meaningless questions are being asked today?
5. Who are the contemporary teachers of legalism? Are they a threat to evangelicalism?
6. What modern sins are contrary to sound doctrine? How can these sins be identified and prevented?
7. In what ways is sharing the gospel a sacred trust? How can that trust be violated?

2

The Conversion of a Legalist

I Timothy 1:12–20

In his zeal for the law, Paul became a legalist in his unsaved Pharisaical life. In fact, he was "more exceedingly zealous of the traditions of [his] fathers" than any of his contemporaries (Gal. 1:14). Like Israel, he had "a zeal of God, but not according to knowledge" (Rom. 10:2). In his attempt to establish a self-righteousness, he was ignorant of divine righteousness and failed to appropriate it (Rom. 10:3).

God, however, saved Paul in spite of his egotistical arrogance, which resulted in the rabid persecution of believers. In fact, Paul's salvation came as a total surprise to the church. When the converted Paul first went to Jerusalem, "they were all afraid of him, and believed not that he was a disciple" (Acts 9:26). Those early Christians must have surmised that the legalistic persecutor was beyond the scope of salvation.

In this section of the epistle, Paul wanted to show Timothy that any sinful person, even a legalist, could be regenerated. As Paul issued the charge, Timothy should seek to evangelize the false teachers.

I. THE TESTIMONY OF PAUL (1:12–17)

The connective "and" (*kai*) links this paragraph with the preceding verse, where Paul mentioned that the gospel had been entrusted to him. The first half of this chapter was objective, dealing with others, whereas this portion is subjective, containing a disclosure about himself.

A. Paul's Present (1:12)

Paul was thankful for his salvation and the opportunity for service. Thankfulness was a constant attitude within him. The verb literally reads, "I am having thanks or grace" (*charin echō*).[1] His gratitude was directed toward "Christ Jesus our Lord." These three names stress His deity, humanity, and redemptive office (cf. 1:1). Paul was thankful for three major reasons.

1. Christ enabled Paul

God's commandments are God's enablements. He never asks a believer to do something without first providing the ability to do it. Christ was the one "who hath enabled" (*tōi endunamōsanti*) Paul. This verb construction points to a time in the apostle's past when Christ placed within Paul the supernatural gift or ability to perform his missionary tasks.[2] This enduement for service, however, remained as an ever-present supply of power. Paul wrote elsewhere, "I can do all things through Christ which strengtheneth [*tōi endunamounti*] me" (Phil. 4:13).[3] The emphasis is on "ability" (*dunamis*) "within" (*en*). No person, no matter how gifted, has an innate or acquired ability to execute the holy stewardship of preaching the gospel. Paul's confession is the admission of all honest servants of God: "Not that we are sufficient of ourselves to think any thing as of ourselves; but our sufficiency is of God" (II Cor. 3:5). Whatever a believer does, he does by the grace of God (I Cor. 15:10). The believer is not passive in the enablement process; rather, he must actively yield his mind and natural talents to the indwelling Christ who manifests Himself through the Christian by the ministry of the Holy Spirit.

1. Present active indicative of *echō*. The concept of thanks is emphasized because the word occurs before the verb. This is the only place in Paul's epistles that he uses this particular construction (cf. Luke 17:9).
2. The verb is an articular participle: aorist, active, dative, masculine, singular.
3. This verb is a present active participle.

2. Christ counted Paul faithful

The basic requirement of spiritual stewardship is faithfulness (I Cor. 4:2). What counts is not ability, but availability and dependability. Human evaluation stresses intelligence and physical appearance, but God looks at the motivations of the heart (I Sam. 16:7; Heb. 4:12).

A faithful person is trustworthy. Actually, the adjective "faithful" (*piston*) and the verb "committed to my trust" (*episteuthēn*) come from the same Greek stem, which stresses the persuasion of the heart, mind, and will.

When and how did Christ deem Paul to be such a faithful person? The time of testing occurred between Paul's conversion (Acts 9:1–5) and his call into missionary service (Acts 13:1–14). This period covered nine years. It began with an appropriate question, answer, and obedient response: "And he trembling and astonished said, Lord, what wilt thou have me to do? And the Lord said unto him, Arise, and go into the city, and it shall be told thee what thou must do" (Acts 9:6). At Damascus, Paul submitted to the ministry of Ananias and was baptized (Acts 9:7–19). He probably then went into seclusion in Arabia (Gal. 1:17). He returned to Damascus, where he conducted an aggressive preaching campaign in the synagogues (Acts 9:20–25). At this time, three years after his conversion, he went to Jerusalem, where he boldly preached (Acts 9:26–29; Gal. 1:17–20). Out of a concern for Paul's safety, the believers sent him back to Tarsus, his hometown (Acts 9:30–31; Gal. 1:21). Years later, Barnabas brought Paul from Tarsus to Syrian Antioch, where they labored together (Acts 11:25–26). These two subsequently carried a gift to the needy believers at Jerusalem (Acts 11:27–30). They later returned to Antioch, where they served with other prophets and teachers (Acts 12:25—13:2).

The result of these years of isolation, subordination, and cooperation was that Paul demonstrated his faithfulness and obedience. He also knew that such divine scrutiny was an ongoing process (I Thess. 2:4).

3. Christ put Paul into the ministry

A leader must first be a follower. He must be mature and experienced (3:6). Paul epitomized those qualities. As a result, Christ put

Paul "into the ministry" (*eis diakonian*). This word can refer either to the technical, administrative office of deacon (3:8) or, generally, to a life of service. In this latter sense, Paul became a minister of the church and of the gospel (Col. 1:23–25). The derivation of the word *deacon* is interesting. It is a compound word, based upon *dia* ("through") and *konis* ("dust"). The imagery suggests a man who moves quickly to perform his tasks and makes a trail of dust by his haste.

The triune God—Father (I Cor. 12:18, 28), Son (1:12), and Spirit (Acts 13:2)—puts a person into the ministry. Although Paul had various types of ministry in his early years as a Christian, the call into missionary service apparently constituted the formal placement in a distinctive ministry. At that time, the Holy Spirit said, "Separate me Barnabas and Saul for the work whereunto I have called them" (Acts 13:2).

B. Paul's Past (1:13–14)

The English relative clause ("who was before") unites Paul's past life with his present thanksgiving for his ministry.[4] Two aspects of his past are enumerated: his unsaved days when he oppressed believers and his conversion.

1. Paul's sinful practice (1:13a)

Paul focused on his relationship to Christ and His church. In his zeal for God, the law, and the traditions of Judaism, he firmly believed that he was doing the service of God by persecuting Christians (cf. John 16:2). To him, this was his finest display of religious devotion, and yet it became a fanatical destruction of the truth. The obstacle to his regeneration was not great moral sin or rebellion, but a proud self-righteousness. Often this type of person becomes more difficult to reach with the gospel than the derelict. What he viewed as right really was wrong and was leading to death (Prov. 14:12; Isa. 64:6).

Paul presented a threefold evaluation of himself. First, he was a

4. The relative clause is actually the translation of an articular participle: *ton proteron onta*.

"blasphemer" (*blasphēmon*). This term derives from *blax* ("stupid") or *blaptō* ("to injure") and *phēmē* ("speech"). To blaspheme is to injure someone with slanderous, stupid words. Blasphemy is a sin that both believers and the unsaved can commit (Matt. 15:19; Col. 3:8). Jesus declared, "All manner of sin and blasphemy shall be forgiven unto men: but the blasphemy against the Holy Ghost shall not be forgiven unto men" (Matt. 12:31). To blaspheme against the Spirit is to claim that Jesus performed His miracles by satanic power rather than by the Spirit (Matt. 12:22–30). Paul had not done that in his hostility toward Christ and the church.

Second, Paul was a "persecutor" (*diōktēn*). Persecution involves pursuit and harassment, both physical and psychological. He "made havock of the church, entering into every house, and haling men and women committed them to prison" (Acts 8:3). The high priest gave him permission to arrest Christians as far away as Damascus (Acts 9:2). Believers were terrified of him; the mere mention of his name struck fear within them (Acts 9:13, 21, 26). He confessed "how that beyond measure [he] persecuted the church of God, and wasted it" (Gal. 1:13; cf. Acts 22:4). When Christ apprehended Paul on the road to Damascus, He asked, "Saul, Saul, why persecutest thou me?" (Acts 9:4). The spiritual union of Christ with His body, the church, meant that the persecution of believers was really a persecution of Christ.

Third, Paul was "injurious" (*hubristēn*). He was a religious bully. D. Edmond Hiebert writes that he was "one whose insolence and contempt of others breaks forth in wanton and outrageous acts."[5] He consented to the death by stoning of Stephen (Acts 8:1), imprisoned some believers (Acts 8:3), and threatened all. Before Herod Agrippa II, he reported, "And I punished them oft in every synagogue, and compelled them to blaspheme; . . . being exceedingly mad against them" (Acts 26:11). This injury involved both physical harm (cf. Acts 27:10) and verbal abuse (cf. Luke 11:45; Acts 14:5). Christ was "spitefully entreated" (Luke 18:32; same word), and so was Paul after his conversion (II Cor. 12:10; I Thess. 2:2).

5. *First Timothy* (Chicago: Moody, 1957), p. 40.

2. *Paul's conversion (1:13b–14)*

The strong adversative conjunction "but" (*alla*) shows the clear contrast between Paul's unsaved life and his salvation experience. He emphasized two aspects about his conversion. First, he "obtained mercy." He literally "was mercied" (*ēleēthēn*).[6] Both daily and saving mercy have their source in God (1:2). All believing sinners have received divine mercy (Rom. 11:31–33; II Cor. 4:1). God withholds from man the judgment he deserves (mercy) and gives to him what he does not deserve (grace).

Paul admitted his sin ("I did it"), but he identified two reasons why God spared him. First, he sinned "ignorantly" (*agnoōn*). He did not deliberately reject grace. The law distinguished between ignorant and presumptuous sin (Num. 15:27-31). Immediate judgment came to the Israelite who sinned presumptuously, but there was opportunity afforded to the repentant offender who sinned ignorantly. Peter claimed that Israel crucified Christ out of ignorance (Acts 3:17; I Cor. 2:8). Second, Paul sinned "in unbelief" (*en apistiai*). The lack of faith is no excuse for sin, but it does explain why Paul sinned.

Second, Paul received "grace" (Eph. 2:8–9). In fact, the grace "was exceeding abundant" (*huperepleonase*) toward him. God's grace has that characteristic—the greater the sin, the more abundant the grace. Paul knew from personal experience that "where sin abounded, grace did much more abound" (Rom. 5:20). This grace was accompanied by "faith and love." By grace, Paul was able to believe on Christ for salvation and love the Savior for His substitutionary sacrifice. All believers must confess, "We love him, because he first loved us" (I John 4:19). The spiritual position of the love "is in Christ Jesus." Justified sinners are accepted in the beloved Savior (Eph. 1:6). In Him, they love and are loved.

C. Paul's Pattern (1:15–16)

In retrospect, Paul perceived the divine reasons behind his conversion. He knew that he was not deserving of salvation because of his sinful past, but he also understood why God had saved him. The

6. Aorist passive indicative.

reasons are introduced by a unique Pauline literary expression: "This is a faithful saying."[7] It is found only five times in the New Testament, and all five are in the pastoral Epistles (1:15; 3:1; 4:9; II Tim. 2:11; Titus 3:8).[8] The adjective "faithful" (*pistos*) stresses that the content of the statement is trustworthy. A person can place his total confidence in that truth. In addition, it is also "worthy of all acceptation" (*pasēs apodochēs axios*). It should receive welcome approval from all people in all situations. There is no moral or rational reason for its rejection. Paul accepted it and proclaimed it. He fully expected that both Timothy and the Ephesian church would likewise respond.

1. A pattern for salvation (1:15)

Salvation has both objective and subjective aspects. The objective aspect stresses the divine provision of salvation through the person and redemptive work of Jesus Christ, whereas the subjective element is the sinner's appropriation of that provision by faith.

Paul stressed three features of the objective aspect. First, he identified the savior ("Christ Jesus"). Christ Himself declared that He is the only one through whom men can come to the Father (John 14:6). Peter dogmatically preached, "Neither is there salvation in any other: for there is none other name under heaven given among men, whereby we must be saved" (Acts 4:12). His very name implies salvation (Matt. 1:21).

Second, Paul pointed to the incarnation ("came into the world"). In order to come *into* the world, Jesus had to be *outside* of it. He was not a mere man, born of two human parents within the world. As God who created man and the universe, He became man through the virgin conception and birth (Gal. 4:4). He was the true light who came into the world, was unrecognized in the world for thirty years, and then was rejected by Israel after His revelation of Himself through His holy life, sermons, and miracles (John 1:9–11). Jesus often dotted His teaching with the words "I am come" (John 5:43; 6:38; 9:39; 10:10). Such expressions point to His conscious preexistence and eternity.

7. The phrase literally reads, "faithful is the word" (*pistos ho logos*).

8. Some commentators believe that these five statements came from some early hymns or doctrinal creeds.

Third, Paul stated the purpose of the incarnation ("to save sinners"). Jesus came to save men, not just to teach them or to live a holy life. Such salvation is accomplished through His substitutionary death on the cross and His subsequent physical resurrection. He came to give "his life a ransom for many" (Matt. 20:28; Luke 19:10).

Within the subjective aspect of salvation, Paul saw himself as a needy sinner ("of whom I am chief"). He placed himself within the group of sinners that Christ came to save ("of whom"; *hōn*).[9] The adjective "first" (*prōtos*) means "first in rank or time," the chief position (Matt. 17:27; 22:38; Acts 28:7). Paul was not the first sinner to be saved in that age, but he did rank himself as the worst sinner among sinners. If anyone deserved judgment in the lake of fire for who he was and what he had done, the apostle firmly believed that he was that person. The present tense of the verb "I am" (*eimi*) shows that he still regarded himself as the chief sinner at the time he wrote the epistle. He was the worst sinner both before and after his conversion. He even intensified the declaration by the use of the personal pronoun (*egō*).[10] When a sinner sees God in all of His absolute holiness and purity, he will then view himself as a totally undeserving wretch (Job 42:5–6; Isa. 6:5; Rev. 1:17). Elsewhere Paul identified himself as "the least of the apostles" (I Cor. 15:9) and as "less than the least of all saints" (Eph. 3:8). The grace of God had changed the proud, assertive Pharisee into the humble, submissive apostle.

2. A pattern for long-suffering (1:16)

Paul knew that the way by which God worked in his life became a "pattern" (*hupotupōsin*). This compound word is composed of *hupo* ("under") and *tupos* ("example, pattern, type"). Paul actually was the basis for the pattern. He was the outline, the sketch, or the prototype. He was the "undertype."

Paul was a pattern in three ways. First, he was the graphic exhibit of the salvation of an undeserving sinner ("Howbeit for this cause I obtained mercy"). This was his second expression of debt to the mercy of God (1:13). If the most undeserving person in the world

9. This Greek relative pronoun is genitive, masculine, plural; its antecedent is the masculine noun "sinners."

10. The verb itself (*eimi*) means "I am."

can become a child of God, then no other sinner is exempt from the divine provision of mercy. It is available to all.

Second, Paul was a type of "longsuffering" (*makrothumian*). The word means that anger or rage (*thumos*) is put far away from (*makran*) the offended person. In dealing with Paul, God manifested "all" long-suffering. After all of Paul's hatred and persecution, the divine intervention on the road to Damascus should have issued in his immediate execution rather than his salvation. God was angry at what Paul had done, but He put His anger far away. Such long-suffering is extended to all men, both to those who will eventually end up in the lake of fire and to the saved (Rom. 9:22; I Peter 3:20). His long-suffering is an expression of His willingness to save, and it should lead men to repentance (Rom. 2:4; II Peter 3:9).

Third, Paul became a pattern for future belief ("to them which should hereafter believe on him to life everlasting"). The verb construction literally reads, "them who are about to believe" (*tōn mellontōn pisteuein.*) If any sinner believes that he is beyond the scope of divine salvation, he should look at the conversion experience of Paul and be encouraged. In one sense, Paul was the worst person who ever lived (1:13), but paradoxically he was also the best man who had ever lived (Phil. 3:4–6). The basis of saving faith is Christ (*ep autōi;* "on him"). Faith must have a solid foundation, and it does in the rock, Christ Jesus. The goal of such faith is eternal life (*zōēn aiōnion*). This is the very life of God that has neither beginning nor ending; but everlasting punishment has a beginning with no ending.

D. Paul's Praise (1:17)

This ascription of praise reads like a benediction, and yet it appears in the first chapter. Paul must have been so overwhelmed by what he had just written that he had to praise God. When he contemplated what he was and what God had done in his life, this spontaneous outburst of worship was both logical and natural.

1. Object of praise

Paul directed his praise to "God" (*theōi*), either to the Father, to Christ, or to the triune God.[11] Both the Father and the Son are

11. No definite article appears with the noun. For this reason, Homer A. Kent, Jr.,

involved in the salvation of men (1:1, 15), and the Holy Spirit is definitely responsible for the work of regeneration (John 3:5; Titus 3:5).

Five characteristics of God are stated. First, He is "the King eternal" (*tōi basilei tōn aiōnōn*). The phrase literally reads "the king of the ages," the only such description of God in the Scriptures. The successive periods of time in the divine redemptive plan are designated as ages. In fact, "eternity" is literally translated as "the ages of the ages" (*tous aiōnas tōn aiōnōn;* "for ever and ever"). God made these ages through Christ (Heb. 1:2). Daniel recognized this sovereign rule of God over history: "And he changeth the times and the seasons: he removeth kings, and setteth up kings" (Dan. 2:21).

Second, God is "immortal" (*aphthartōi*). Only God is innately incorruptible. This term is used elsewhere of the incorruptible crown that a believer can obtain (I Cor. 9:25), the resurrection body (I Cor. 15:52), the heavenly inheritance (I Peter 1:4), the seed of regeneration (I Peter 1:23), and the inner virtue of a meek and quiet spirit (I Peter 3:4). As applied to God, "He is exempt from that wear and waste and final perishing; that *phthora,* which time, and sin working in time, bring about in all which is outside of Him."[12]

Third, God is "invisible" (*aoratōi*). This adjective is used four times of God (1:17; Rom. 1:20; Col. 1:15; Heb. 11:27) and once of created things (Col. 1:16). God is "spirit" (John 4:24). As such, He is not physical, material, or corporeal. Man has only seen God as He has chosen to reveal Himself through theophanies and in the incarnate Son, Jesus Christ (John 1:18).

Fourth, God is unique. He is the only (*monōi*) God (I Cor. 8:6). This adjective forms part of the noun *monotheism.* Other gods do not exist, even though sinful man, deluded by Satan and demons, thinks that they do.

Fifth, God is "wise" (*sophōi*). God has never learned, nor will He ever. He is omniscient. He knows all things, both actual and possible, eternally. His wisdom and knowledge, which created the

---

believes that it refers to the trinitarian God. See *The Pastoral Epistles* (Chicago: Moody, 1979), p. 94.

12. Robert C. Trench, *Synonyms of the New Testament* (Grand Rapids: Eerdmans, 1950), p. 254.

plan of redemption, are unsearchable (Rom. 11:33; 16:27). Through the church, the "manifold wisdom of God" is being revealed to the angels (Eph. 3:10).

2. Description of praise

Two points of eternal praise are enumerated. First, all believers should ascribe "honour" (*timē*) to God. They should recognize Him to be the most precious being in the universe. Without Him, they would have nothing (Matt. 16:26).

Second, a believer must render "glory" (*doxa*) to God. The glory of God is the outward manifestation of what He really is. Believers glorify Him when they reveal in their lives the fruit of the Spirit (Gal. 5:22-23). Men must see what God has done in and through redeemed sinners.

II. THE RESPONSIBILITY OF TIMOTHY (1:18-20)

The apostle again focused on the obligation of Timothy to the original charge ("this charge"; see 1:3, 5). The account of Paul's salvation was an illustration, not a distraction. Its purpose was to encourage the young associate in the performance of his tasks at Ephesus.

A. Receive the Charge (1:18-19a)

The verb "commit" (*paratithemai*) literally means "to place beside." It is used of setting food before others (Mark 6:41; 8:6-7; Luke 10:8; 11:6; Acts 16:34; I Cor. 10:27), of the commitment of the spirit to God (Luke 23:46; Acts 20:32; I Peter 4:19), and of the proclamation of spiritual teaching (Matt. 13:24; Acts 17:3). As the disciples passed on the bread and fish that Christ had placed in their hands, so Timothy was to pass on to the church and to faithful men the doctrinal concepts of Paul (II Tim. 2:2). The term also had a meaning taken from the business world. It denoted a deposit left for safekeeping (Luke 12:48; II Tim. 1:12). Jesus declared that "to whom men have committed [same word] much, of him they will ask the more" (Luke 12:48). The apostle expected much from his associate in whom he had invested much time and energy in discipleship.

1. Standard of the charge

The basis for giving the charge is introduced by the words "according to" (*kata*). When Paul and Silas came into the region of southern Galatia during the second missionary journey, the apostle determined to have Timothy join the team (Acts 16:3). Timothy had been "well reported of by the brethren" in that area (Acts 16:2). At that time, God imparted to Timothy a special gift of ministry through the instrumentality of Paul (4:14; II Tim. 1:6). Both Paul and the Galatian elders laid hands on Timothy. This occasion was marked by supernatural prophetic utterances that identified Timothy's future usefulness to the work of God ("the prophecies which went before on thee"; cf. 4:14).

2. Purpose of the charge

Both Paul and Timothy were spiritual soldiers (II Tim. 2:3–4). Paul wanted his spiritual subordinate to "war a good warfare" (*strateuēi en autais tēn kalēn strateian*). The emphasis of this military term is on the entire war fought throughout the lifetime, not just an isolated battle.[13] The English word *strategy* is based upon this Greek term. To fight the good fight, Timothy had to remember the prophecies whereby the leaders had placed confidence in him ("by them").[14] The war must be conducted in the realm of spiritual truth, which has been supernaturally revealed.

3. Concomitants of the charge

A believer must contend for the faith without being contentious (Jude 3). He must engage in war with the proper weapons. He not only must *fight* correctly, but also must *be* correct. The participle "holding" (*echōn*)[15] stressed the constant responsibility of Timothy.

13. The verb is in the present tense.

14. The pronoun "them" (*autais*) is feminine plural, in agreement with its antecedent, "prophecies" (*prophēteias*).

15. Present active participle.

Two qualities were indicated. First, Timothy needed to hold "faith" (*pistin*). The absence of the definite article *the* places emphasis upon personal, subjective trust. Believers must walk and fight by faith (1:5; 3:9).

Second, Timothy needed to have a "good conscience" (cf. 1:5; 3:9). Someone has said that faith is a pure liquid and a good conscience is the glass that holds it. All spiritual ministries must be done without reproach. A minister should know nothing about himself that might disqualify him from service (I Cor. 4:3–4).

B. Beware of Enemies (1:19b–20)

The occasion for the charge was the presence of false teachers within the church (1:3).

1. Sin of the false teachers (1:19b)

Paul switched the language of the spiritual metaphor from that of the army to that of the navy. He traveled by sea often and was shipwrecked on at least four occasions (Acts 27:40–44; II Cor. 11:25). He thus was familiar with nautical terms.

Two aspects of these teachers' sin are set forth. First, they "put away" (*apōsamenoi*) a good conscience. The relative pronoun "which" (*hēn*) refers back to the conscience.[16] Bad behavior leads to bad doctrine. Their determination to forsake a moral conscience that manifested the goodness of God soon developed into an apostate position. In a sense, they pulled up their moral anchor and caused their lives to be tossed by the winds and waves of heresy (cf. the language of Acts 27:40–41).

Second, the false teachers destroyed their faith ("concerning faith have made shipwreck"). The verb (*enauagēsan*) is based upon the noun *ship* (*naus*) and the verb *to break in pieces* (*agnumi*). They shattered their lives upon the rocks of error.

2. Names of the false teachers (1:20a)

Two of the false leaders are named. There were others ("of whom is"). The first was "Hymenaeus." Mentioned only twice in the New

16. Both words are feminine singular.

Testament, he and Philetus "concerning the truth have erred, saying that the resurrection is past already; and overthrow the faith of some" (II Tim. 2:18).

The second was "Alexander." Several men bear this name in the New Testament: the son of Simon the Cyrenian, who carried the cross of Jesus (Mark 15:21); a relative of the Jewish high priest (Acts 4:6); and a Jewish resident of Ephesus (Acts 19:33). It is very plausible that this third person is the same Alexander the coppersmith who harmed Paul and who was a problem member of the church at Ephesus (II Tim. 4:14).

3. Discipline of the false teachers (1:20b)

The radical step of deliverance to Satan was an apostolic prerogative, not given to any church or to any other individual. Paul said, ". . . whom *I* have delivered unto Satan" (italics added). The powers of binding and loosing (Matt. 16:19) and of the remission and retention of sins (John 20:23) were given only to the apostles and were seldom used by them (Acts 5:1–10; 13:8–11). Such a deliverance involves neither a consignment to Hades or the lake of fire nor a loss of salvation. Outside the church is the world, the sphere of satanic dominion (Eph. 2:12; Col. 1:13; I John 5:19). It is in that realm that Paul wanted to see the two adversaries chastised.

The purpose of the deliverance was corrective, not punitive ("that they may learn not to blaspheme"). The verb "learn" (*paideuthōsi*) refers to the discipline of erring children. Paul wanted the men to repent and to be restored into proper moral and doctrinal fellowship. Apparently they were not chastened by this corrective procedure and persisted in their opposition to Paul and the truth (II Tim. 2:17; 4:14; cf. Heb. 12:11).

Questions for Discussion

1. By what means does God enable believers to perform spiritual tasks? Relate such ability to native talent and human effort.
2. How can believers determine whether a pastoral candidate has been faithful? What are the marks of faithfulness for a church member?

3. What is the ministry? Can a distinction be made between a lay and a professional ministry?

4. How can men commit sin ignorantly? Is ignorance an excuse?

5. Can a person deny the deity of Jesus Christ or His virgin birth and be saved? What are the minimum doctrinal points that are necessary for saving faith?

6. How does God manifest His long-suffering? How do sinners irritate God?

7. How can men put away a good conscience? How can this be prevented?

3

The Necessity of Prayer

I Timothy 2:1-7

The first section of the epistle dealt with Paul's personal charge to Timothy about the legalists (1). In the second major portion of the book, the apostle gave instructions about the public life of the local church. These instructions covered five areas: the place of prayer in the assembly (2:1–7), the relationship of women to men (2:8–15), the qualifications of the pastor (3:1–7), the requirements for a deacon (3:8–13), and the nature of the local church (3:14–16).

The phrase "first of all" (*prōton pantōn*) introduced the first subject of many to be discussed. Donald Guthrie, however, claims that it denoted "primacy of importance."[1] Warren W. Wiersbe thinks prayer was the "most important [element] in the public worship of the church."[2]

The forceful "I exhort" (*parakalō*) indicates a strong, constant appeal. Behind this phrase was the delegated authority of the apostle. Public prayer in the local church is not optional; rather, it is obligatory. It should and must be exercised.

The disciples asked Jesus how to pray (Luke 11:1). Prayer needs direction and instruction. In this passage, Paul outlined the content of corporate prayer by believers.

I. THE BENEFIT OF THE SAVED (2:1–3)

Jesus prayed for Himself before He prayed for others (John 17). It is not wrong for a believer to pray for himself or to pray for himself

1. *The Pastoral Epistles,* Tyndale Bible Commentary (Grand Rapids: Eerdmans, 1972), p. 69.
2. *Be Faithful* (Wheaton, IL: Victor Books, 1981), p. 27.

as he intercedes for others. There is a valid factor of self-interest in prayer that should not be criticized.

A. Types of Prayer (2:1a)

Jesus taught that prayer involves relationship, reverence, submission, dependence, forgiveness, and trust (Luke 11:1–4). These attitudes must be manifested through the four types of prayer listed.

1. Supplications

The focus of "supplications" (*deēseis*) is upon the needs of others and self. The word stresses the idea of intense entreaty, even to the point of begging. Its urgency can be seen by its use in the request of the leper (Luke 5:12), the demoniac (Luke 8:28, 38), the father of a possessed child (Luke 9:38, 40), and the distressed Simon (Acts 8:24). Such prayer marked Jesus (Luke 22:32), the disciples (Acts 4:31), Cornelius (Acts 10:2), Paul (Rom. 1:10), Zacharias (Luke 1:13), Anna (Luke 2:37), and the disciples of John the Baptist (Luke 5:33). James argued, "The effectual fervent prayer [same word] of a righteous man availeth much" (James 5:16). Such supplications are heard and answered by God (I Peter 3:12).

2. Prayers

Supplications (*deēseis*) can be directed to both God and man, but "prayers" (*proseuchas*) are addressed only to God. This term is the most general word used for prayer in the New Testament. The word implies worship, adoration, and reverence, and is all-inclusive.

3. Intercessions

The term translated as "intercessions" (*enteuxeis*) occurs only twice in the New Testament, both times in this epistle (2:1; 4:5). It is based upon the verb *entugchanō,* which is found five times (Acts 25:24; Rom. 8:27, 34; 11:2; Heb. 7:25). The verb means "to fall in with a person, to draw close to him so as to enter into familiar speech and communion with him."[3] The Jewish leaders, both at

3. Robert C. Trench, *Synonyms of the New Testament* (Grand Rapids: Eerdmans, 1950), p. 190.

Jerusalem and at Caesarea, "dealt" (*enetuchon*) with the Roman governor Festus for the execution of Paul (Acts 25:24). A contemporary parallel is the activity of political lobbyists. Both Jesus Christ in heaven (Rom. 8:34; Heb. 7:25) and the Holy Spirit within the believer (Rom. 8:27) make intercession for the child of God. They share an intrapersonal oneness and familiarity with the Father. In *enteuxeis,* a Christian gets close to God before he makes his request. It is an "approach to God in free and familiar prayer."[4]

4. Thanksgiving

Prayer and the "giving of thanks" (*eucharistias*) are inseparable (Dan. 6:10; Phil. 4:6). Paul counseled, "Pray without ceasing. In every thing give thanks: for this is the will of God in Christ Jesus concerning you" (I Thess. 5:17-18). Thanksgiving prevents selfishness and coldness in prayer. The word means "to say something good (*eu*) to the one who has bestowed gracious gifts" (*charis*) upon you. A believer must be thankful to God for His dealings with him in his past, present, and future. He must thank God for His answer to prayer even before that answer is received. A mark of ecclesiastical apostasy in the last times will be an "unthankful" spirit (II Tim. 3:2).

B. Objects of Prayer (2:1b-2a)

The two groups who are the objects of believers' prayers are indicated by the preposition "for" (*huper*). Although the word "for" occurs three times in the English translation, it appears only twice in the Greek text. Both groups should be the recipients of all four types of prayer. The verb "be made" (*poieisthai*)[5] shows that such prayer should be a constant priority within the church. It should be exercised at each service, not just on national holidays.

1. All men (2:1b)

The first group is very general. The classification "all men" (*pantōn anthrōpōn*) includes the saved and the unsaved, men and

4. Kenneth S. Wuest, *Word Studies in the Greek New Testament,* vol. 12, *The Pastoral Epistles* (Grand Rapids: Eerdmans, 1952), p. 39.

5. Present passive infinitive.

women, bond and free. No racial, political, economic, or social class is excluded. The word envelops men of no influence as well as those with much power.

2. Government leaders (2:2a)

Sincere Christians first recognize that God has ordained the human institution of government to control lawlessness within a sinful world (Rom. 13:1-6). Jesus taught that there is no innate conflict between God and the state (Matt. 22:15–22). Problems of conscience and obedience develop when the state moves into an area not assigned to it by God (Acts 4:19; 5:29). In allegiance to the sovereign authority of God over the delegated authority of the government, believers should render honor and support to their leaders (Rom. 13:7). Peter tersely commanded, "Honour all men. Love the brotherhood. Fear God. Honour the king" (I Peter 2:17).

Believers also acknowledge that God is in absolute control of the affairs of nations. God removes and replaces rulers (Dan. 2:21). They perform His pleasure (Isa. 44:28). Within His permissive will, such nations and rulers are morally responsible for wars and assassinations. God, however, works in and through the actions of men, whether those deeds are good or evil, to accomplish His ultimate will (Eph. 1:11).

Believers confess that all governments will eventually surrender their delegated authority to Jesus Christ at His return to the earth to establish His eternal kingdom (Rev. 11:15; 19:11–16).

For these three reasons, Paul charged that prayer should be offered for the second group, which has two subcategories: "for kings, and for all that are in authority" (*huper basileōn kai pantōn tōn en huperochēi ontōn*).[6] The first word, "kings," refers to national leaders. For each kingdom, there is a king. The plural noun, therefore, refers to more than the imperial power of the Roman Caesar. Within the empire, land areas were still ruled by recognized kings who were loyal to the emperor. Outside of the empire, in other parts of the world, existed other kingdoms.

The second word applies to all lesser government officials of various ranks. Few believers ever have direct relationships with kings.

6. Note the single use of the preposition *huper* with the two groups.

Their conflicts with government usually come at the local level. Regardless, believers have a responsibility to pray for those who presently "are" (*ontōn*)[7] in leadership.

C. Purposes of Prayer (2:2b–3)

The two purposes of prayer in this passage are indicated by the conjunctions "that" (*hina*) and "for" (*gar*). These purposes relate to both the believer and God.

1. Pursuit of godliness (2:2b)

The verb "may lead" (*diagōmen*)[8] refers to the daily lifestyle. The benefit to the church also extended to Paul (note "we"). It is translated as "living" in the only other occurrence of the verb (Titus 3:3).

Two features of the pursuit of godliness are mentioned. First, the object is a "quiet and peaceable life." The adjective "quiet" (*ēremon*), found only here, denotes the outward political and social situation. The word connotes the absence of international war, the cessation of internal anarchy, and freedom from persecution. The term "peaceable" (*hēsuchion*) emphasizes that believers will not need to protest verbally any mistreatment. The same word is used of godly women who are to learn in "silence" within the church and who have a "quiet" spirit in the home (2:11, 12; I Peter 3:4). The aroused Jewish multitude kept "silence" (Acts 22:2; same word) when the accused Paul began to speak in Hebrew. Believers should work at their secular jobs with such "quietness" (II Thess. 3:12). Outward pressures bring internal distress, which often issues in outbursts of complaint and protest. This type of social environment is not conducive to the development of the Christian life.

Second, the sphere of pursuit is "in all godliness and honesty." The first term (*eusebeiai*) points to the religious devotion of the believer to God. There is no difference between the sacred and the secular for the committed Christian. He seeks to glorify God in all aspects of life (I Cor. 10:31). The latter term (*semnotēti*) describes that which is honorable, serious, and grave. The word indicates

7. Present participle.
8. Present active subjunctive.

grace and dignity. The concept goes beyond mere honesty, the integrity of one's actions, to the general character of the person himself. It has special relevance to interpersonal relationships as seen in deacons (3:8), the wives of deacons (3:11), and aged men (Titus 2:2). Both Titus (Titus 2:7) and the pastor (3:4) must manifest such spiritual gravity and decorum.

2. Pleasure of God (2:3)

The demonstrative pronoun "this" (*touto*) points back to the command and the content of the preceding two verses. Such prayer has two divinely approved qualities. First, it is "good" (*kalon*). D. Edmond Hiebert observes that "it is excellent in its nature and characteristics and is well adapted to its ends."[9] This adjective actually is a key word in the epistle, used eighteen times (1:8, 18; 2:3; 3:1, 2, 7, 13; 4:4, 6 [twice]; 5:4, 10, 25; 6:12 [twice], 13, 18, 19).

Second, such prayer is "acceptable" (*apodekton*), a word used only twice in the New Testament (2:3; 5:4). This adjective is based upon a verb (*apodechomai*) that stresses the idea of a warm, joyful reception (Luke 8:40; Acts 2:41; 15:4; 18:27; 24:3; 28:30). Prayer thus is welcomed by God and will be answered by Him.

Prayer is good and acceptable "in the sight of God our Saviour" (*enōpion tou sōtēros hēmōn theou*). There is only one God, and only He can save.

Later Paul used this same descriptive phrase in promoting the financial support of widows by believing members of her family (5:4).

II. THE BENEFIT OF THE LOST (2:4-7)

Prayer for the lost is based upon the redemptive program of God. The mention of the divine title "Saviour" caused Paul to introduce a relative clause that began with the pronoun "who" (*hos*). This feature forms the transition from the first section of this passage to the next. The second half of the passage reveals a genuine concern for the lost by the Father, the Son, and the apostle.

9. *First Timothy* (Chicago: Moody, 1957), p. 52.

A. God's Will and Salvation (2:4)

The will of God is both simple and complex; it is single yet multiple. He works "all things after the counsel [*boulēn*] of his own will" (*thelēmatos;* Eph. 1:11). All things, including creation, sin, redemption, and judgment, are encompassed by the divine decree. For purposes of understanding, however, the will of God can be classified in three ways. His decretive will expresses His unconditional purpose; it gives Him pleasure and it is always carried out because it is dependent only upon Him for its fulfillment (Isa. 14:24, 27). Creation is an illustration of the decretive will (Gen. 1:3–4). His preceptive will states His conditional purpose. The performance of His moral will is dependent upon the obedience of man for its fulfillment. The Ten Commandments and the desire to save reveal God's moral, preceptive will. Man must will to do what God has willed. Unfortunately, both believers and nonbelievers have willed not to obey God. His permissive will allows sin and evil to occur. God is not morally responsible for the sinful actions of men and the consequences of those acts. Such rebellion gives God no pleasure (Ps. 81:12; Acts 14:16; Rom. 1:24).

The will of God in this passage points to His moral, preceptive will. The verb "will" (*thelei*) indicates a "desire springing out of the emotions or inclinations, rather than out of deliberation (*boulomai*)."[10] Actually, the distinction between the two words for "will" (*thelō* and *boulomai*) should not be imposed upon this passage. Elsewhere, Peter wrote that God was not "willing [*boulomenos*] that any should perish, but that all should come to repentance" (II Peter 3:9). Both words, therefore, manifest God's intense concern for the salvation of the lost.

God's preceptive, redemptive will has two purposes. They are indicated by the use of two infinitives.

1. God wills all men to be saved

The verse literally reads, "who wills all men to be saved" (*hos pantas anthrōpous thelei sōthēnai*). Paul did not write that God

10. Homer A. Kent, Jr., *The Pastoral Epistles* (Chicago: Moody, 1979), p. 103. Wuest, *The Pastoral Epistles,* p. 40, concurs.

wills to save all men. The infinitive is in the passive voice, not in the active. If God had willed to save all, then all would be saved. This, however, contradicts the clear teaching of Scripture that unsaved men will be banished to eternal torment in the lake of fire (Rev. 20:11–15). The passive voice shows that man must will to be saved. God does not impose His redemptive, preceptive will upon unwilling sinners. To obey the appeal to believe, man must actively exercise his will (Acts 16:31).

The group "all men" includes the entire world of lost humanity (cf. 2:1). Believers can pray for all men to be saved because divine provision has been made for all to be saved (John 3:16; 12:32; I John 2:2).

2. God wills all men to come to the truth

In His moral, preceptive will, God also wills all men "to come unto the knowledge of the truth." The infinitive (*elthein*)[11] stresses the nonrepeatable event of conversion. Christ issued His gracious invitation: "Come unto me, all ye that labour and are heavy laden, and I will give you rest" (Matt. 11:28). That appeal can be either accepted or rejected. At the same time, the sovereign purpose of God in unconditional election is in effect. Jesus also said, "No man can come to me, except the Father which hath sent me draw him" (John 6:44). At the moment of faith and regeneration, the paradoxical truth of divine choice and human responsibility are both active. God works in and through the will of man to gain the assent of that will without violating its moral accountability.

The goal is the "knowledge of the truth." The noun "knowledge" (*epignōsin*) denotes a thorough understanding. Sinners do not become believers through ignorance. They must have moral perception of some basic redemptive facts. Those facts are contained in the "truth" (*alētheias*), which is outlined in the next three verses: the oneness of God, the necessity of a divine-human mediator, the death and resurrection of Jesus Christ, and the appropriation of salvation by faith.

Redemptive truth centers in Jesus Christ. He declared, "I am the

11. Aorist active infinitive.

way, the truth, and the life: no man cometh unto the Father, but by me" (John 14:6). Knowledge of such truth sets men free from their bondage to sin (John 8:32; II Thess. 2:13–14). The possession of eternal life is synonymous with knowing God and Christ through a redemptive experience (John 17:3). Paul was willing to repudiate his proud, self-righteous life for "the excellency of the knowledge of Christ Jesus" (Phil. 3:8).

B. Christ's Work and Salvation (2:5–6)

The conjunction "for" (*gar*) introduces the explanation of redemptive truth. The emphasis also switches from the Father to the Son. As a mediator, the attention is on the Son's person, whereas as a ransom, the focus is on His work.

1. Christ is the mediator (2:5)

Three concepts are enumerated. First, there is only "one God." The gods that sinful men worship simply do not exist (I Cor. 8:5–6). If many gods did exist, then there would be different approaches to those various gods. There would consequently be many ways of salvation. Since only one God exists, He alone has the sovereign prerogative to determine the proper access into His presence (Deut. 6:4–5).

Second, there is only "one mediator between God and men." A mediator is an umpire. Wuest observes that a mediator is "one who intervenes between two, either in order to make or restore peace and friendship, or to form a compact or ratify a covenant."[12] The necessity of a mediator can be seen in the moral gulf between a holy God and a sinful humanity. When God created the first human pair, there was instant fellowship; however, in their disobedience, they fled from the presence of God. Man, not God, needs reconciliation (Rom. 5:10; II Cor. 5:19).

Third, the one mediator is the "man Christ Jesus." The absence of the definite article *the* before the noun "man" stresses that Christ became a perfect and complete man.[13] He has the same human

12. *The Pastoral Epistles,* p. 41.
13. The definite article is not in the Greek text.

nature as all other members of the human race (Heb. 2:14, 16). A sinful nature is not an innate part of the human nature. Adam was a perfect man before he obtained a sinful nature at his fall. Christ thus is very man of very man. Men needed a man to represent them, and that man is Christ. The phrase does not imply a denial of His deity. Since He "came into" the world, He existed as God prior to His incarnation (1:15). The phrase affirms that the mediator had to be both divine and human in order to represent the interests of the two parties. The only one who could bring both God and man together Himself had to be both God and man.

In his concern, Job confessed, "For he is not a man, as I am, that I should answer him, and we should come together in judgment. Neither is there any daysman betwixt us, that might lay his hand upon us both" (Job 9:32–33). His desired "daysman" was Christ, who placed His hands on both God and man. Christ thus became the mediator (*mesitēs*) of the new covenant ratified by His shed blood (Heb. 8:6; 9:15; 12:24).

2. Christ is the ransom (2:6)

Five truths about the redemptive price can be gleaned from this verse. First, the ransom is a gift. The verb "gave" (*ho dous*)[14] looks back to the death of Christ on the cross. God the Father gave His Son out of love (John 3:16), and so did the Son. His death was voluntary, not compulsory.

Second, Christ gave "himself" (*heauton*). He is both the giver and the gift. At the cross, He was both the priest and the sacrifice. In the construction of the church, He as the builder laid Himself as the foundation stone. He "loved the church, and gave himself for it" (Eph. 5:25).

Third, Christ is the "ransom" (*antilutron*). The doctrine of biblical redemption draws much of its language from terms used in the ancient slave markets. Sinners thus are slaves to sin (John 8:34). Christ bought (*agorazō*)[15] sinners or paid the purchase price for all sinful humanity (I Cor. 6:20; II Peter 2:1; Rev. 5:9). He also bought men out of (*exagorazō*) their spiritual bondage (Gal. 3:13; 4:5).

14. Aorist active participle.
15. The noun *agora* means "market."

They were redeemed from both the law and its curse. He then set them free (*lutroō;* Titus 2:14; I Peter 1:18). The term "ransom" is a compound word, built upon this third concept (*lutron*) and the preposition "in the place of" (*anti*). Although this is the only verse where the noun occurs in the New Testament, the combination does appear elsewhere. Christ declared that He came to give his life "a ransom for many" (*lutron anti pollōn;* Matt. 20:28; Mark 10:45).

Fourth, Christ is a substitute "for all" (*huper pantōn*). The two Greek prepositions (*anti* and *huper*) definitely show that Christ died in behalf of all and in the place of all. The universal scope of the statement is supported by the term "all," which is used throughout this passage to refer to all people (2:1, 4, 6). There is a difference, however, between the provision of universal redemption and its individual appropriation by faith.

Fifth, Christ's death fulfilled the prophetic program of redemption ("to be testified in due time"). In the Garden of Eden, God announced that the seed of the woman would bruise the head of Satan (Gen. 3:15). The line of the promised redeemer thus extended from Adam to Abraham to David to Christ (Luke 3:23–38). In the fullness of time, God then "sent forth his Son, made of a woman, made under the law, To redeem them that were under the law, that we might receive the adoption of sons" (Gal. 4:4–5). The right person came at the right time in the right way to do the right thing. What was written under divine inspiration came to pass.

C. Paul's Ministry and Salvation (2:7)

The transitional word "whereunto" can literally be translated "unto which" (*eis ho*). The relative pronoun (*ho*) refers to the testimony (*to marturion;* 2:6). Paul was "ordained" (*etethēn egō*) to be a public witness to the redemptive program of God. He earlier discussed his placement in the gospel ministry (1:12).

Between the will of God and the faith of men stands the necessary witness of a concerned Christian. Paul knew this truth, and thus burdened with an evangelistic concern, he "strived to preach the gospel, not where Christ was named" (Rom. 15:20). God had ordained both the means and the end of the gospel. In this verse, Paul described his role in three ways.

1. Paul was a preacher

As a "preacher" (*kērux*), Paul preached the word (II Tim. 4:2). He understood the logic of evangelism: "For whosoever shall call upon the name of the Lord shall be saved. How then shall they call on him in whom they have not believed? and how shall they believe in him of whom they have not heard? and how shall they hear without a preacher? And how shall they preach, except they be sent?" (Rom. 10:13–15). He declared what God had revealed about the program of salvation and what He had done in the apostle's life.

Wuest states, "The Imperial Herald would enter a town in behalf of the Emperor, and make a public proclamation of the message which his Sovereign ordered him to give, doing so with such formality, gravity, and authority as must be needed."[16] Throughout his three missionary journeys, Paul did just that.

2. Paul was an apostle

Paul knew that he was a genuine "apostle" (*apostolos*), one who had seen the resurrected Christ and who had been commissioned by Him to preach and lay the foundation of the church age (I Cor. 9:1–2; Eph. 2:20).

Timothy also knew that Paul was an apostle. Thus the emphatic affirmation was expressed for the benefit of the Ephesian church and the adversaries ("I speak the truth in Christ, and lie not").[17] Constrained by the Holy Spirit, he often had to appeal to God for His confirmation of the apostolic witness (Rom. 9:1; II Cor. 11:31; Gal. 1:20).

3. Paul was a teacher

Paul catechized after he evangelized (see Matt. 28:18–20). The process of discipleship involves constant instruction.

The object of Paul's teaching was the "Gentiles" (*ethnōn*). Although he ministered in synagogues to numerous Jewish audiences, his main effort was with the pagan Gentile world (Acts 13:46–48; 14:27). He stated that he was "the minister of Jesus Christ

16. *The Pastoral Epistles*, p. 44.
17. The phrase "in Christ" is not in the critical Greek text.

to the Gentiles, ministering the gospel of God, that the offering up of the Gentiles might be acceptable, being sanctified by the Holy Ghost" (Rom. 15:16). The other apostles recognized his unique ministry to the non-Jewish world (Gal. 2:7–9).

The sphere of Paul's teaching was "in faith and verity" (*en pistei kai alētheiai*). He wanted people both to believe and to understand what he proclaimed. The word "verity" is actually translated as "truth" (2:4). It is the "belief of the truth" that saves a sinner (II Thess. 2:13). Faith is the means, and truth is the content. The legalists, unfortunately, were proclaiming a religion of works and error.

Questions for Discussion

1. How often do congregations pray for government officials? What content should be included in the prayers?

2. What are the advantages of living in a society governed by law? Compare the level of Christianity within free countries and the Communist world: personal development, missions, and giving.

3. Should Christians ever protest the evil in the world? their mistreatment by society? How does suffering for the sake of righteousness relate to this?

4. What is unlimited atonement? limited atonement? Relate these concepts to orthodoxy and evangelism.

5. What must a sinner believe in order to be saved? What essential points of biblical doctrine must be understood and accepted?

6. How can Jesus Christ be both divine and human? How do the two natures function within His person?

7. To what extent are all believers ordained to be witnesses of the gospel? Is there any difference between a professional and a lay ministry to the lost?

4

The Roles of Men and Women

I Timothy 2:8–15

The first topic of local church order to be discussed is prayer (2:1-7). The second major subject is the relationship of the man to the woman (2:8–15). The two sections both begin with the conjunction "therefore" (*oun;* 2:1, 8). Both sections start with personal appeals: "I exhort" (*parakalō;* 2:1) and "I will" (*boulomai;* 2:8).

I. MEN (2:8)

Paul's expression of his will comes very close to a direct command. He also used this literary device to issue directives on other topics: the deportment of younger widows (5:14) and the preaching responsibility of Titus (Titus 3:8). This volitional verb (*boulomai*) seems to be stronger than the other (*thelō*) in that it originates from the mind rather than the emotions.[1] Obedience to the apostolic counsel, therefore, was not optional; rather, it was required.

The term "men" (*tous andras*) refers to the male in contrast to the female (*gunē*). In the first section, both sexes were included in the generic word "men" (*anthrōpōn;* 2:1, 4, 5).

A. The Need to Pray

1. At all times

The verb "pray" (*proseuchesthai*)[2] stresses constant prayer. Since Paul did not use the titles of the church officers (pastor and deacon),

1. Kenneth S. Wuest, *Word Studies in the Greek New Testament,* vol. 12, *The Pastoral Epistles* (Grand Rapids: Eerdmans, 1952), p. 45.
2. Present middle infinitive, deponent.

all male believers were eligible to participate in public prayer. D. Edmond Hiebert actually argues, "The men only are to lead in public prayer."[3] That strict interpretation is difficult to maintain dogmatically. All believers, including women, must grow in the spiritual life. Women as well as men need to "pray without ceasing" (I Thess. 5:17). Prayer and prophecy by women within the apostolic church were approved by Paul under certain guidelines of subordination to the men (I Cor. 11:5). If such commanded prayer was to be exercised from the pulpit by an authoritative church officer, then naturally it could be performed only by a male.

2. In all places

The adverbial phrase ("every where") literally reads "in every place" (*en panti topōi*). The interpretation could be limited to mean every place of meeting or every house church within the city of Ephesus. The general view extends the meaning to include both public and private prayer in all geographical locations (I Cor. 1:2; I Thess. 1:8).

B. The Attitude in Prayer

It is not enough to pray; it must be done in the right way. Prayer must issue from the sanctified, humble heart of a believer in fellowship with God.

1. Holy hands

Does the phrase "lifting up holy hands" indicate a physical posture or an inner spiritual attitude? It is true that both David and Solomon prayed with arms stretched out toward the presence of God (I Kings 8:22; Ps. 28:2; 63:4; 134:2). It would be difficult, however, to prove that they always prayed in this position. Others have prayed in various physical postures: Daniel was on his knees facing toward Jerusalem (Dan. 6:10); David sat before the Lord (II Sam. 7:18); Eliezer bowed his head in worship (Gen. 24:26); Abraham fell on his face on the ground (Gen. 17:3); the repentant

3. *First Timothy* (Chicago: Moody, 1957), p. 57.

publican stood with his eyes downcast (Luke 18:13); and Jesus lifted His eyes toward heaven in His intercession (John 17:1). Such postures were not planned or ritualistic; rather, they spontaneously manifested the prayerful impulse of the moment.

Hands, in themselves, are neither "holy" (*hosious*) nor unholy. They are simply parts of the human anatomy. If the elevation of hands were necessary, then amputees without arms or hands would be in an impossible situation. Rather, the "hands" (*cheiras*) are "symbolic of daily life."[4] Holy hands thus indicate an unpolluted spiritual life. David equated his righteousness with the cleanness of his hands (II Sam. 22:21). He later asked this rhetorical question: "Who shall ascend into the hill of the LORD? or who shall stand in his holy place? He that hath clean hands, and a pure heart; who hath not lifted up his soul unto vanity, nor sworn deceitfully" (Ps. 24:3–4).

Haggai argued that a sinful heart automatically defiles any religious work of the hands (Hag. 2:11–14). Prayer, in itself, does not make the petitioner clean; rather, a pure heart makes prayer acceptable to God. The psalmist recognized this basic truth: "If I regard iniquity in my heart, the Lord will not hear me" (Ps. 66:18).

2. Without wrath and doubting

This phrase partly explains what is involved in having "holy hands." The words show that a believer must be right in his relationships both to man and to God.

The first term, "wrath" (*orgēs*), focuses on emotional anger vented on men, both believers and the unsaved. Even though the petitioner has been wronged by others, he must put off that natural, sinful response of anger before he goes into the presence of God (Col. 3:8). Jesus warned that such inner fury must be replaced by a spirit of reconciliation (Matt. 5:21–26). A believer must be "slow to wrath: For the wrath of man worketh not the righteousness of God" (James 1:19–20).

The second term, "doubting" (*dialogismou*), is the opposite of inner confidence. Instead of having faith, a Christian doubts when he has skeptical criticism of God's control over his life. He carries

4. Homer A. Kent, Jr., *The Pastoral Epistles* (Chicago: Moody, 1979), p. 108.

on a mental dialogue about the outcome of his prayer. It is possible that the disputation may extend to arguments with fellow believers about the programs within the local church. In that sense, doubting disrupts the spiritual unity and the effectiveness of the body of Christ. Paul cautioned, "Do all things without murmurings and disputings" (Phil. 2:14; same word).

II. WOMEN (2:9-15)

The major portion of this passage is devoted to the deportment and spiritual function of "women" (*tas gunaikas*). This term refers to adult women who are single, married, or widowed.

The transitional phrase "in like manner" (*hōsautōs*) relates this section to the original main verb "I will" (2:8). Thus Paul stated, "I will . . . that women adorn themselves. . . ."

A. Clothing (2:9-10)

1. The directive

Two features of the command are given. First, the women have the responsibility to clothe themselves properly. The reflexive pronoun (*heautas*) indicates that the women make the choices. The husband is not given the prerogative to dress his wife according to his concept, nor do women dictate to other women what they should wear. The verb "adorn" (*kosmein*)[5] also stresses this duty. The verb is related to the noun *world* (*kosmos*).[6] The world, as the planned creation of God, reveals beauty, purpose, design, and order. Everything was in its proper place fulfilling its assigned function. It thus was good in His sight (Gen. 1:4, 10, 12, 18, 21, 25, 31). The verb is also used of the garnishing of sepulchres (Matt. 23:29), the furnishing of a house (Matt. 12:44), the trimming of oil lamps (Matt. 25:7), the embellishment of the temple (Luke 21:5), and the beautification of the holy city (Rev. 21:19).

5. Present active infinitive.
6. The word *cosmetics* is also based upon the verb.

Second, the women should adorn themselves "in modest apparel." The word "modest" (*kosmiōi*) actually is derived from the verb "adorn" (*kosmein*). Modest clothing, therefore, is apparel suitable for the occasion. It is planned, orderly, and beautiful. No piece of clothing that is necessary should be missing. Every item should be in its proper place.

2. The description

The term "apparel" (*katastolēi*), found only here in the New Testament, refers to that which is visible and material, although some scholars believe that it also refers to the deportment of the women.[7] The emphasis of the passage, of course, is that the outward should manifest the inward. Each should be in harmony with the other.

Two features about the dress are discussed. The first is positive and emphasizes spiritual clothing. Throughout the Scriptures, believers are exhorted to put off the rags of the old sinful life and to put on the robes of the sanctified life (Col. 3:8–14). Four qualities of virtuous demeanor are given. The first is "shamefacedness" (*aidous*). Translated as "reverence" in its only other use (Heb. 12:28), it connotes respect, dignity, and a proper humility in the presence of others. The second is "sobriety" (*sōphrosunēs*), a compound noun that literally means a "sound mind." The concept of "sound" (*sō*) comes from the verb *to save* (*sōzō*). A saved person should thus think and act like a saved person (Acts 26:25; I Tim. 2:9, 15; 3:2; Titus 1:8; 2:2, 4). A Christian woman should practice sound judgment, self-control, and a seriousness of spiritual purpose when she selects and wears her clothing. The third feature is to wear that "which becometh women professing godliness." A godly woman cannot clothe herself with the "attire of a harlot" (Prov. 7:10). As the holy city is "prepared as a bride adorned for her husband" (Rev. 21:2), so a godly woman will want to be spiritually attractive to Christ. The fourth quality is "good works" (*ergōn agathōn*), which correspond to the innate goodness of God. She should be known "not in what she herself puts on, but in the loving service she gives

7. Hiebert, *First Timothy*, p. 58; Donald Guthrie, *The Pastoral Epistles*, Tyndale Bible Commentary (Grand Rapids: Eerdmans, 1972), p. 74.

out."[8] Dorcas was a perfect illustration, "full of good works and almsdeeds which she did" (Acts 9:36). Other examples were Anna (Luke 2:36–38), Lydia (Acts 16:14), Priscilla (Acts 18:1–3), and Phebe (Rom. 16:1). The Book of Proverbs gives an extensive description of the virtuous wife and mother who will be praised by her family and friends (Prov. 31:10–31).

The second feature of the dress is negative and looks at the physical items. Paul wanted the godly woman to be known for who she is, not for what she wears. Three aspects of physical attractiveness are mentioned: hair, jewelry, and clothing (I Peter 3:1–6). The "broided hair" (*plegmasin*) was hair interwoven with ribbons and jewels, which caused it to shine. In this way, a woman increased her own glory in the presence of others. Instead of drawing attention to themselves, Paul counseled women to cover their hair as a cultural badge of subordination to their husbands (I Cor. 11:5–6). The "gold" and "pearls" accented certain parts of the body or pieces of apparel. The "costly array" (*himatismōi polutelei*) drew attention to the woman's financial status.

The main issue is modest apparel, clothing suitable for a Christian woman in a local church. Solomon said with amusement, "As a jewel of gold in a swine's snout, so is a fair woman which is without discretion" (Prov. 11:22). The inward and the outward characteristics should match in order to have proper or modest apparel.

B. Relationship to Men (2:11–12)

There is a notable switch from the plural ("women") to the singular ("woman") in this section. From the general realm of feminine deportment Paul advanced to the individual responsibilities within the leadership of the church.

1. A woman should learn

Learning is obligatory, not optional. Paul issued a command to the woman to learn ("Let the woman learn").[9] The verb (*manthanetō*) is the basis for the word *disciple* (*mathētēs*). This verb

8. Guthrie, *The Pastoral Epistles*, p. 75.

9. The English word "let" does not imply permission. This is a general command issued in the third person rather than in the direct second person.

denotes constant learning of spiritual truth imparted by God through gifted teachers.[10] Christ commanded the apostles to teach or disciple all nations (Matt. 28:19). This process involves evangelization, baptism, and instruction (Matt. 28:18–20; II Tim. 2:2).

A woman's learning must take place in two spheres. First, she must learn "in silence" (*en hēsuchiai*). This silence does not imply the absence of sound. She may sing, discuss, pray, and teach children and other women in the church. The silence involves the absence of vocal conflict in debate and protest. The Jewish believers at Jerusalem criticized Peter for preaching to the Gentiles in the house of Cornelius, but after he explained the operation of God, they "held their peace [*hēsuchasan;* verb base for "silence"], and glorified God, saying, Then hath God also to the Gentiles granted repentance unto life" (Acts 11:18). They spoke, but yet they were in silence inasmuch as they ended their protests. Some of Paul's friends tried to persuade him not to go to Jerusalem, but they finally "ceased" (same word) their argumentation, "saying, The will of the Lord be done" (Acts 21:14). The admonition for women to "keep silence [*sigatōsan;* different word] in the churches" refers to the ministry of judicial discernment, to the asking of questions, and possibly to the speaking in tongues (I Cor. 14:34).

Second, a woman must learn "with all subjection." Subjection or submission is not subjugation. The former stems from a voluntary spirit, whereas the latter is forced upon unwilling hearts. The term "subjection" (*hupotagēi*) literally means "under rank." Such rank "has to do with order and authority, and not with value or ability."[11] Within the home and the church, the woman must yield to the functional headship of the man (I Cor. 11:3; Eph. 5:22; Col. 3:18). There must be reciprocal personal submission between the man and the woman (Eph. 5:21). Both are personally equal and both are positionally one in Christ, but there is a functional order appointed by God for the performance of functions within the family and the assembly. The woman must joyfully accept this role of subordination without emotional and vocal restlessness.

10. The verb is a present active imperative.
11. Warren W. Wiersbe, *Be Faithful* (Wheaton, IL: Victor Books, 1981), p. 34.

2. A woman should not teach men

The verb (*epitrepō;* "I suffer not") deals with permission (Matt. 8:21; Mark 10:4; John 19:38). Speaking as an apostle invested with divinely delegated authority (1:1), Paul did not give a woman permission to teach a man.

The infinitive "to teach" (*didaskein*) means "to be a teacher."[12] A woman can teach a man both in the home and in the church about particular issues, and a man can definitely learn from the feminine perspective. However, she cannot have the formal position as a permanent, authoritative teacher in the church. Paul was a teacher (2:7), equipped by the Spirit with the gift of teaching (Rom. 12:7), and given by Christ to the church for administrative duties (Eph. 4:11–12). Only males qualify for the position of the bishop-pastor-elder who must be "apt to teach" (3:2).

3. A woman should not have authority over men

A woman also could not have an authoritative position over men in the church. She could not issue pronouncements of doctrine and practice that would have to be obeyed by men in order to avoid ecclesiastical discipline. The verb (*authentein*) means "to have the mastery of" or "to lord it over another." The translation "usurp" goes beyond the nature of the word. Usurped authority over men of course is innately wrong, but even delegated authority, authorized by a congregational vote, would violate the principle of spiritual headship. No board of elders or congregation has the biblical right to assign such administrative powers to a woman. It is impossible for a man to be the head of his wife in the home and then to have that same woman be the head over her husband in the church. The church and the family function under the same concepts of headship. Again, the present tense of the infinitive looks at the permanent position of an authoritative church officer.

4. A woman should be in silence

A woman should rest quietly and confidently in the role assigned to her by God. No vocal or unexpressed protests should originate

12. Present active infinitive. The aorist tense would have been used if a woman could never teach in any situation.

within her. This second mention of "silence" (2:11) stresses the importance of her attitude. Peter claimed that "a meek and quiet spirit" within a woman was a valuable asset before God and man (I Peter 3:4).

C. Order of Man and Woman (2:13–14)

There is a difference between headship and dictatorship. There is an equality of persons within the trinitarian God. The Father, the Son, and the Spirit share the same divine essence. Within the redemptive program, however, the Father is greater than the Son in that the sender is greater than the one sent (John 13:16; 14:28). Paul thus stated that God the Father is the head of God the Son (I Cor. 11:3).

By analogy, the apostle asserted that the head of the woman is the man (I Cor. 11:3). There is an ontological oneness and equality within the human race, but there is a practical order for the execution of the divine program for the home and the church.

In this passage, Paul set forth two major reasons for the man's headship, which establishes his leadership role within the church.

1. Priority in creation (2:13)

The male human was created by God before the female human. Paul simply stated this fact: "For Adam was first formed, then Eve." The conjunction "for" (*gar*) introduced the explanation why women should not authoritatively teach men.

Priority does not imply superiority; rather, it indicates authority over the family. In the families of ancient Israel, the firstborn male received a double portion of the inheritance and leadership of the family at the death of the father.

In the record of creation, God "formed man of the dust of the ground, and breathed into his nostrils the breath of life; and man became a living soul" (Gen. 2:7). Adam then began to care for the garden (Gen. 2:8–17). God knew that Adam needed a female companion so He formed Eve out of Adam's side (Gen. 2:18–25). In the order of creation, Eve came after Adam, although she was potentially and genetically present in Adam. Moses wrote, "So God created *man* in his own image, in the image of God created he *him;* male and female created he them" (Gen. 1:27; italics added).

Both the man and the woman are in the image of God. They are moral persons whose intellect, emotion, and will are found within their spiritual selves. Paul wrote, "For the man is not of the woman; but the woman of the man. Neither was the man created for the woman; but the woman for the man" (I Cor. 11:8-9). God created Eve to meet the needs of Adam. This factor, along with the priority in creation, established the male as the administrative leader of the couple and the family.

2. *Result of the transgression (2:14)*

At this point in his argument, Paul discussed the cause and the effect of the original sin committed in the Garden of Eden by Adam and Eve. He made three observations. First, Adam "was not deceived" (*ēpatēthē*). He was not deceived by Eve or by Satan who is the deceiver (*planaō*) of all nations (Rev. 20:3). Deception can come through riches (Matt. 13:22), intense desires (Eph. 4:22), philosophy (Col. 2:8), sin (Heb. 3:13), self-indulgence (II Peter 2:13), pride (I Cor. 3:18), and heretical doctrine (II Thess. 2:3). A man can deceive himself (I Cor. 3:18) or be deceived by another. In the great tribulation, the man of sin will deceive the lost (II Thess. 2:10). However, both believers and the unsaved can be deceived by Satan. Adam entered into his sin of disobedience with a conscious understanding of his actions (Gen. 3:6, 11). In that sense, he was "more culpable"[13] than Eve. Sin and death, therefore, are related to Adam rather than to Eve. Paul thus commented, "Wherefore, as by one man sin entered into the world, and death by sin; and so death passed upon all men, for that all have sinned" (Rom. 5:12). Although Eve chronologically sinned before Adam, he bears the responsibility as the head or representative of the human race because he sinned presumptuously. In his sin, he also violated the principle of headship bestowed on him through the priority of creation. God stated the two reasons for his condemnation: "Because thou hast hearkened unto the voice of thy wife, and hast eaten of the tree . . ." (Gen. 3:17).

13. Guthrie, *The Pastoral Epistles,* p. 77.

Second, Eve was "deceived" (*apatētheisa*).[14] She was thoroughly beguiled by Satan (II Cor. 11:3). The serpent deceived her by the lust of the flesh, the lust of the eyes, and the pride of life (Gen. 3:6; I John 2:16). At the time God confronted Eve with her sin, she admitted that Satan had beguiled her (Gen. 3:13). Guthrie argues that one reason for male leadership is "the greater aptitude of the weaker sex to be led astray."[15] This rare interpretation would be difficult to maintain with any degree of dogmatism.

Third, Eve "was in the transgression." The verb "was" (*gegone*)[16] stresses the abiding result of her initial act of disobedience. God pronounced this judgment upon Eve and upon all female descendants: "I will greatly multiply thy sorrow and thy conception; in sorrow thou shalt bring forth children; and thy desire shall be to thy husband, and he shall rule over thee" (Gen. 3:16). There would be physical pain in the delivery of babies and emotional pain through miscarriages, infant deaths, and birth defects. One major result of her sin is the rulership or headship of the man over her. As long as the judgment of God rests upon the human race, the principle of male headship must be accepted. At physical death or the return of Christ, the operation of this principle will cease.

Women thus should not authoritatively teach or lead men in ecclesiastical or family matters because of the priority of male creation and the results of the female's role in the original sin.

D. Salvation of Women (2:15)

The conjunction "notwithstanding" (*de*) contrasts what a woman can do (2:15) with what she cannot do (2:12). The woman can have a meaningful life of spiritual purpose full of joy and satisfaction. The verb "saved" (*sōthēsetai*) does not always mean salvation from sin and eternal punishment. It can mean deliverance from disease (Mark 5:34), imminent physical death (Acts 27:20), and doctrinal and moral error (4:16).

14. Aorist passive participle. The critical Greek text adds the prefix *ex* to the verb with the meaning "thoroughly deceived."

15. *The Pastoral Epistles*, p. 77.

16. Perfect active indicative.

1. Means of a woman's salvation

A woman shall be saved "in childbearing." The phrase literally reads "through the childbearing" (*dia tēs teknogonias*). Paul used this word later in his counsel for younger widows to marry and to bear children (5:14).

Various interpretations of this unusual phrase have been given. Some are discussed here. First, a woman will physically survive the trauma of childbirth; however, both mothers and babies have died at this critical time.

Second, a woman can receive spiritual salvation through childbirth. If a woman dies in the process of bearing a child, then she will automatically go to heaven. However, sinners are justified by faith in Christ, not by any works of righteousness, including the worthy deed of childbirth.

Third, a common view is that the woman will experience salvation though *the* childbearing. The use of the definite article points to the incarnation and virgin birth of Christ through Mary. Eve was saved by faith in the promised seed of the woman, namely, Christ (Gen. 3:15). Thus, women today can be saved from sin through faith in Christ. They will also be saved from the effects of the curses on women at the return of the Savior.

Fourth, a woman will be saved from spiritual uselessness through the acceptance of God's program for the godly woman.[17] A woman can have authoritative leadership in the home that she guides (5:14; Prov. 31:10–31). She can rule over her children and teach them. She can have a ministry of teaching other women (Titus 2:4). The man needs her support and counsel in order to carry out his leadership responsibilities. Paul thus wrote, "Nevertheless neither is the man without the woman, neither the woman without the man, in the Lord" (I Cor. 11:11).

2. Conditions of a woman's salvation

The condition of spiritual effectiveness is introduced by the particle "if" (*ean*). The prerequisite is that "they continue" (*meinō-*

17. Author's view.

sin). There is an obvious switch from the singular to the plural here. To whom does the pronoun "they" refer? It can refer to the women,[18] to the woman and child, or to the wife and her husband.[19] The last view seems to be the most plausible, since both parents have a spiritual responsibility within the home (Eph. 6:4; Col. 3:21). It is difficult for a godly woman to do her appointed task when she has no support from either an unsaved husband or a believing husband who has forsaken his duties.

Four areas of spiritual vitality must be maintained. First, the couple must abide in "faith." Both must walk by faith and trust God.

Second, the couple must continue in "charity." They must love each other (Eph. 5:25; Titus 2:4), their children, and their Savior God.

Third, the couple must advance in "holiness" (*hagiasmōi*). They must separate themselves from worldly lusts and actively pursue godliness.

Fourth, the couple must abide "with sobriety" (*meta sōphrosunēs*). They must manifest sound judgment in the development of their marriage and the upbringing of their family (cf. 2:9).

Questions for Discussion

1. What is the contemporary role of male leadership in the prayer life of the local church? Why do men shrink from this responsibility?
2. Why do believers doubt when they pray? How can this problem be solved?
3. What is modest apparel? in church? in the home? in recreational activities? Do the fashions of the world need to be modified?
4. How much money and time should be devoted to cosmetics? to jewelry? to a wardrobe? to membership in a spa?
5. What good works should mark the Christian woman of today? How should she be praised for them?

18. Hiebert, *First Timothy*, p. 62.
19. Wiersbe, *Be Faithful*, p. 38, and Wuest, *The Pastoral Epistles*, p. 51.

6. How can women teach men without violating the principle of male leadership? Why are some men unwilling to learn from women?

7. How can the husband and the wife cooperate in their parental roles? When do marital and parental roles conflict?

5

The Qualifications of a Pastor

I Timothy 3:1–7

This new section is introduced with a popular expression of that day: "This is a true saying." A literal translation is "faithful is the word" (*pistos ho logos*). This word is trustworthy. A person can believe it and communicate it to others without fear of contradiction. Paul used the saying often in the pastoral Epistles (1:15; 3:1; 4:9; II Tim. 2:11; Titus 3:8).

I. THE POSITION OF THE PASTOR (3:1)

A local church has two administrative offices: the pastor and the deacon (3:1, 8; Phil. 1:1). In the first century, other gifted men functioned with spiritual authority. These official positions ceased when the foundation of the church age had been laid and when special revelation, both oral and written, ended with the completion of the New Testament canon. These temporary positions were apostles (Eph. 2:20; 4:11), prophets, like Agabus (Acts 21:10–11; Eph. 2:20; 4:11), and evangelists, like Philip (Acts 21:8; Eph. 4:11). The men who held these positions actually had administrative leadership over churches, pastors, and deacons. Their demise has left the authority for faith and practice in the Scriptures, which are protected and propagated through the local churches as they are led by pastors and deacons (3:15).

God appointed a select group of men to the positions of apostle, prophet, and evangelist (2:7; Gal. 1:1). No believer could aspire to or work into such positions; however, a male Christian can "desire" (*oregetai*) the office of a pastor. The verb means "to covet, to reach out after, to stretch oneself toward, to aspire to" (cf. 6:10; Heb. 11:16). The second verb, translated as "desireth" (*epithumei*), stresses an intense emotional desire (Gal. 5:17). Both verbs reveal that any dedicated, qualified believer (*tis;* "man") can become eligible for the position. He can claim the Old Testament promise: "Delight thyself also in the LORD; and he shall give thee the desires of thine heart. Commit thy way unto the LORD; trust also in him; and he shall bring it to pass" (Ps. 37:4–5). The local church today determines whether a believer has met the qualifications and whether he should be elevated to an administrative position over its members.

A. Terms That Describe the Office

Three terms are used to describe the chief presiding officer of the local church: "bishop" (*episkopos*), "elder" (*presbuteros*), and "pastor" (*poimēn*). That the terms are used interchangeably or synonymously of the same group is demonstrated in the following passages. After Paul summoned the Ephesian elders (*presbuterous*), he said to them, "Take heed therefore unto yourselves, and to all the flock, over the which the Holy Ghost hath made you overseers [*episkopous*], to feed [*poimainein*] the church of God" (Acts 20:17, 28). Peter also made the same identification when he addressed the elders (*presbuterous*): "Feed [*poimanate*] the flock of God which is among you, taking the oversight [*episkopountes*] thereof, not by constraint, but willingly; not for filthy lucre, but of a ready mind" (I Peter 5:1–2). Two of the terms are equated in the Pastorals (3:1–2; cf. 5:17; Titus 1:5, 7).

1. Bishop

The phrase "the office of a bishop" is the translation of one Greek word (*episkopēs*). It has the same noun stem but a different gender ending from the term "bishop" (*episkopon*).[1] The former refers to the office, position, or function, whereas the latter points to the person or officer.

The term is based upon a compound Greek word that means

1. The former is feminine and the latter is masculine.

"oversight" (*epi,* "over," and *skopos,* "sight").[2] It is derived from two verbs (*episkopeō* and *episkeptomai*) that mean "to visit" or "to look upon," to inspect as an overseer or a superintendent, or in modern terms, a foreman.

In a nontechnical sense, the title is applied to Jesus Christ, who is "the Shepherd and Bishop of your souls" (I Peter 2:25). Christ, as its living head, oversees the universal church (Eph. 1:22–23), just as the bishop oversees a local church. The term was also applied to the apostolic oversight, which Judas forfeited by his unbelief and apostasy (Acts 1:20). This word is used five times of the main church leader (3:1, 2; Acts 20:28; Phil. 1:1; Titus 1:7).

2. Elder

The title *elder* (*presbuteros*) reflects the "maturity and dignity of the office."[3] This word is related to *presbutēs,* an adjective that signifies old age (Luke 1:18; Titus 2:2; Philem. 9). It is even translated with this meaning (5:1–2). It is also related to the concept of being an ambassador (*presbeuō;* Luke 14:32; 19:14; II Cor. 5:20; Eph. 6:20).

In the Gospels and Acts, the plural "elders" is a designation of Jewish religious rulers who are set in contrast to the priests and the scribes (Mark 14:43). Jewish men who held this influential position within the Sanhedrin were relatively old. Their age, power, and status brought them honor and respect.

Local churches were organized with elders in each one (Acts 14:23; James 5:14). In the church at Jerusalem, a distinction was made among the apostles, elders, and brethren (Acts 15:23). Later, however, both Peter and John identified themselves also as elders (I Peter 5:1; II John 1).

In the Book of Revelation, the term is applied to a symbolic group of redeemed people (Rev. 4:4; 5:8).

No age requirement was set for the position of the main church officer, but the concept of spiritual seniority and respect is contained within the term.

2. The denominational title *Episcopalian* is based upon this word.
3. Homer A. Kent, Jr., *The Pastoral Epistles* (Chicago: Moody, 1979), p. 122.

3. Pastor

In the Old Testament, only Jeremiah employed the term "pastors" for the religious leaders of the people (Jer. 2:8; 3:15; 10:21; 12:10; 17:16; 22:22; 23:1–2). The English translation "pastor" (*poimēn*) is found only once in the New Testament (Eph. 4:11). In that passage, the gifts of pastoring and teaching are united in one person (*tous poimenas kai didaskalous*).[4]

The Greek word is usually translated as "shepherd." It refers to a shepherd of a flock of sheep (Luke 2:8). The terms "flock" (*poimnē;* Luke 2:8) and "little flock" (*poimnion;* Luke 12:32) are related to it.

Believers are symbolized as the spiritual flock of God, equated to the universal church (John 10:16) and to the local church (I Peter 5:2).

Christ said, "I am the good shepherd: the good shepherd giveth his life for the sheep" (John 10:11). Writers later called Him the "great shepherd of the sheep" (Heb. 13:20; cf. Ps. 23:1) and the "Shepherd and Bishop of your souls" (I Peter 2:25). In the future, He will rule or shepherd His redeemed people (Rev. 7:17), Israel (Matt. 2:6), and the nations (Rev. 19:15).

The duty of the pastor usually consists of feeding (*poimainē*) the people of God with biblical, spiritual food (John 21:16; Acts 20:28; I Peter 5:2). The chief Shepherd, in His absence from earth, has committed the pastoral care of His sheep to undershepherds who will give an account of their ministries at the return of Christ (I Peter 5:4).

B. Function of the Office

The office of a bishop-pastor-elder is a "good work" (*kalou ergou*). The office involves work, but it is a wholesome, beneficial labor. It deals with people and their needs: spiritual, social, familial, psychological, and financial. A good work, therefore, requires a good person.

4. The Granville Sharp rule of grammar applies here. One article appears with two nouns joined by a conjunction.

1. Tasks

First, a pastor is to shepherd and to feed. The main responsibility here is the supply of spiritual nourishment through biblical instruction. A pastor must be a teacher, first and foremost (Eph. 4:11; I Tim. 3:2). Pastoral care has three goals delineated by Jesus Christ Himself: to teach the immature or new Christians (John 21:15), to teach adult believers (John 21:17), and to guide all the flock (John 21:16).[5]

Second, the responsibility of the "bishop" is to render oversight, to see that the work of the local church is done correctly by the members who have been trained by him, and to guard the church from the inroads of error.

Third, the term "elder" refers to the individual's position and to the respect others give him.

2. Concepts

In the second century, a distinction was made between a bishop and an elder, with the former being acknowledged as superior to the latter. There is no biblical support, however, for making such a distinction. In addition, there is no indication that a bishop had oversight over a group of churches in the first century.

The use of the plural (5:17) shows that one church could have more than one bishop-pastor-elder. Since one city might contain several house churches (Acts 2:46), this could indicate that each assembly had one bishop. All believers within one community constituted one church regardless of their respective meeting places. They were both organically and organizationally joined together. The situation does not prevail today because of the various denominational groupings.

No prescribed number of bishops within a local church was set. The number of pastors depended on each church's needs and on the availability of qualified men. In this passage, there is a notable contrast between the single bishop (3:1–2) and the multiple deacons (3:8).

5. This distinction is clear in the Greek text.

Only men were appointed to the position of bishop. The designated qualifications could apply only to men (3:2–7).[6] No woman could have administrative headship over the man in either the home or the church (2:11–15; I Cor. 11:2–16).

Because of the time and effort involved in their work, the bishops were to be supported financially by the church (5:17–18; I Peter 5:2). The amount was to be in direct proportion to their effort and success (5:17).

II. THE QUALIFICATIONS OF A PASTOR (3:2–7)

The conjunction "then" (*oun*) joins the desire for the office of pastor with the qualifications for that position. The verb "must be" (*dei . . . einai*) stresses the moral and logical necessity for such specific prerequisites.

The adjective "blameless" (*anepilēmpton*) serves as a general description of the person's life.[7] The long list of virtuous qualities simply defines what a blameless life is. The adjective literally means "not to be taken upon." A pastor must be without reproach in all areas of his conduct and belief. No just cause for censure or criticism should be able to be proven against him. He must be "unrebukeable" (6:14; same word).

A. Marital Qualification (3:2a)

A pastor must be "the husband of one wife." Literally, this phrase reads "one-woman man" (*mias gunaikos andra*). Those three words have engendered much controversy and differing interpretations. Some of the most common interpretations are listed.

First, some Roman Catholic scholars see this as a marriage to the church. To them, celibacy is an ecclesiastical law added to assist discipline in the life.

Second, this qualification is a prohibition against bigamy or

6. The adjectives are all in the masculine gender.

7. This adjective is used only three times in the New Testament, all in I Timothy (3:2; 5:7; 6:14).

polygamy. If this were so, then widows could not be supported by the church if they were involved in polyandry (5:9).

Third, a pastor must be married. A single man who has never married does not qualify. If that were correct, then the phrase would have read "a husband of a wife." The addition of "one" has significance. Such faulty logic would also imply that a married man without children would not qualify either (3:4).

Fourth, a pastor can have only one wife in his lifetime.[8] If his wife dies, he cannot remarry if he wants to retain his position. Marriage after the death of a spouse, however, is nowhere prohibited or criticized in either Testament (Rom. 7:1–3). There is no indication that a pastor would lose his blameless character if he chose to remarry after the death of his wife. Companionship is preferable to loneliness in the will of God (Gen. 2:18).

Fifth, the best view is that the pastoral candidate cannot have more than one living wife. The phrase therefore prohibits divorce and remarriage.[9] Kent states, "Consequently, when men were to be considered for this high office, there must be no record of divorce or other marital infidelity in the candidate, even before his conversion."[10] Sexual sin committed after marriage would also disqualify the pastor from maintaining his position. Even though he could be forgiven and restored to his wife and church family, he would no longer be blameless in his marital life. All must recognize that there is only one woman to whom he is devoted.

B. Personal Qualifications (3:2b)

Five characteristics are set forth in this list of personal virtues that must be apparent to the observer.

1. Vigilant

A "vigilant" (*nēphalion*) person is one who is temperate, wise, and cautious. He is alert to what is going on around him, and yet he

8. Kenneth S. Wuest, *Word Studies in the Greek New Testament,* vol. 12, *The Pastoral Epistles* (Grand Rapids: Eerdmans, 1952), p. 54.

9. Warren W. Wiersbe, *Be Faithful* (Wheaton, IL: Victor Books, 1981), p. 42.

10. *The Pastoral Epistles,* p. 129.

is calm. The word is derived from a term meaning "wineless." Such a person's mind and judgment are absolutely clear.

Elsewhere, the adjective is translated as "sober" (3:11; Titus 2:2). It is based upon a verb (*nēphō*) that is written as either "be sober" (I Thess. 5:6, 8; I Peter 1:13; 5:8) or "watch" (II Tim. 4:5; I Peter 4:7).

2. Sober

The adjective "sober" (*sōphrona*) literally means "sound-minded." Its four occurrences are translated as "sober" (3:2; Titus 1:8), "temperate" (Titus 2:2), and "discreet" (Titus 2:5). Its noun form previously appeared as "sobriety" (2:9, 15).

A sober person thinks straight. He is not mentally confused. When the demoniac was cured by Christ, he was "in his right mind" (*sōphroneō;* Mark 5:15). A serious attitude, however, does not imply the absence of a sense of humor.

3. Orderly

The phrase "of good behavior" (*kosmion*) is the same word seen earlier as "modest" (2:9). The pastor must be an organized person. His life should exhibit planning and purpose. He should know what he wants to do and how he can do it.

4. Hospitable

The phrase "given to hospitality" literally means "a lover of strangers" (*philoxenon*). The pastor must be friendly, warm, and responsive to new people whom he meets. He should be able to welcome them into the church family and into his own home (Rom. 12:13; Titus 1:8; Heb. 13:2). He must exercise hospitality "without grudging" (I Peter 4:9).

5. Capable teacher

A pastor must be "apt to teach" (*didaktikon;* cf. II Tim. 2:24). The office of bishop demands the dual responsibilities of pastoring and teaching (Eph. 4:11). He must have the gift of teaching, imparted by the Spirit of God (Rom. 12:7; I Cor. 12:28–29). He must be "holding fast the faithful word as he hath been taught, that he may be able by sound doctrine both to exhort and to convince the gainsayers" (Titus 1:9). A teacher must first be taught (II Tim. 2:2). He must have both the understanding of biblical truth and the necessary oral and verbal skills to communicate that truth.

C. Social Qualifications (3:3)

The first three qualifications are stated negatively; the latter three begin with a positive note, followed by two more negative assertions.

1. No affinity for wine

The phrase "not given to wine" literally reads "not beside wine" (*mē paroinon*). The pastor is not a constant drinker (Titus 1:7). In that culture, wine was an acceptable beverage. As the alcoholic content of the wine increased, the wine was mixed with water to decrease its intoxicating effects.[11] The pastor must have no affinity for wine, regardless of its age or alcoholic content. Donald Guthrie believes that the phrase "implies drunkenness."[12] A Nazirite vowed to drink no wine in his dedication to God (Num. 6:3). In a contemporary culture infatuated with alcoholic beverages, a pastor can do no less. There are many blameless beverages open to his selection today.

2. Not violent

The listing of winedrinking and violent behavior ("no striker") is no coincidence (Titus 1:7). The former in excess usually leads to the latter. A candidate must be neither belligerent nor quarrelsome. He must not use physical force to get his way or to eliminate his enemies.

3. Not greedy of money

A pastor must "not be greedy of filthy lucre" (*mē aischrokerdē*).[13] Money, in itself, is neither good nor bad. What makes it evil is its

11. Robert H. Stein, "Wine-Drinking in New Testament Times," *Christianity Today*, June 20, 1975, pp. 9–11.
12. *The Pastoral Epistles*, Tyndale Bible Commentary (Grand Rapids: Eerdmans, 1972), p. 81.
13. This phrase does not appear in the critical Greek text.

misuse or abuse. The "love of money" causes all kinds of evil (6:10). The pastor must not be in the ministry for what he can gain financially. He must not view the ministry as a means of making a living (Titus 1:7; I Peter 5:2). He should preach out of spiritual compulsion, ready to give, not to get (I Cor. 9:16; I Peter 5:2).

4. Gentle

A pastor must be gentle (*epieikē*), a better rendering than "patient." (See II Corinthians 10:1; Titus 3:2; James 3:17; and II Peter 2:18, where this word is translated as "gentle.") A pastor must be actively considerate toward those who have mistreated him and who differ with his policies. He must exercise magnanimous forbearance. All believers should manifest their "moderation" (same word) to all men (Phil. 4:5). He must return good for evil (Rom. 12:21).

5. Peaceful

The pastor must not be a "brawler." The word (*amachon*) literally means "without war." He must not be contentious, causing factions to arise; rather, he must be committed to the ministry of reconciliation. He must "fight the good fight of faith" (6:12) without being an uncompromising, adamant pugilist.

6. Not covetous

The Greek word (*aphilarguron*) literally means "not a lover of silver." The pastor must be a lover of the Master, not of money (6:10). One writer cautioned, "Let your conversation be without covetousness [same word]; and be content with such things as ye have" (Heb. 13:5). No avarice should mark the pastor's life.

D. Family Qualifications (3:4–5)

A pastor deals with all types of people found within society. The family is the basic unit of any society. Family members have different sexes, ages, jobs, and concerns. In order to minister effectively to their needs, a pastor must himself be a successful parent. His family management must provide a leadership model that other families in the church can emulate.

1. The pastor must rule well (3:4a)

The pastor must be "one that ruleth well his own house." The verb (*proistamenon*) means "to stand before." He stands before, not above. He presides over the affairs of the family. He thus is a manager, a governor, an administrator, or a director. He stands before his wife and children to lead and guide them, not to shout authoritarian decrees at them.

A pastor must rule "well" (*kalōs*). The method is as important as the action. His management should be beautiful and excellent. The present tense of the verb indicates that his administration should constantly be of superior quality. The members of the church should want to have families like his.

2. The pastor must parent well (3:4b)

If a pastor has children, his relationship to his children must be examined. A childless husband is no more disqualified from the office than is a single male candidate. The "children" (*tekna*) are those who have not yet attained adulthood (Gal. 4:1–3). The qualities of children who are married or who are single, responsible adults should not affect the candidate's eligibility for the office.

Three features of the pastor's fatherhood are presented. First, his control of his children must be constant. The present tense of the verb "having" (*echonta*) stresses the habit of his life.

Second, the children must be "in subjection" (*en hupotagēi*). The children must yield to the headship of their father just as the wife submits to her husband (2:11). Paul wrote elsewhere that a pastor should have "faithful children not accused of riot or unruly" (Titus 1:6). The children must be believers who are not insubordinate.

Third, the pastor must parent "with all gravity" (*meta pasēs semnotētos*). This prepositional phrase probably refers to the father rather than the children. It is a characteristic of adults that should be manifested by deacons (3:8), the wives of deacons (3:11), and aged men (Titus 2:2). Believers should live with such honest dignity (2:2) and should think upon "honest" things (Phil. 4:8; same word). The pastoral candidate must obey the general command to parents:

"Provoke not your children to wrath: but bring them up in the nurture and admonition of the Lord" (Eph. 6:4; cf. Col. 3:21).

3. The pastor must care for the church (3:5)

The logic of this parenthetical question is unrefutable: "For if a man know not how to rule his own house, how shall he take care of the church of God?" The answer is obvious. It is impossible for a poor father to become a good pastor. It is possible for a good father to become a poor pastor, but only good fathers can qualify for the position of spiritual leadership.

The verb "take care" (*epimelēsetai*) is used elsewhere only of the good Samaritan and the innkeeper who both met the needs of the injured pilgrim (Luke 10:34–35).

E. Spiritual Qualifications (3:6–7)

The next two qualities deal with the issues of time and impact. Both qualifications involve experience in spiritual growth and outreach.

1. Mature believer (3:6)

The pastor must not be a "novice" (*neophuton*).[14] The Greek term, transliterated into English as "neophyte," literally means a "new plant." In the parable of the wheat and the tares, God planted seed that sprang up as wheat. In its early stages of growth, the wheat could hardly be distinguished from the tares that Satan had sown in the same field (Matt. 13:24–30, 36–43). The separation of the two had to wait until both had grown to maturity at harvest time. In like manner, a pastoral candidate must not be a new convert. He must give evidence of spiritual growth and maturity.

Two dangers for a premature appointment to a position of leadership are given. First, the pastor could be "lifted up with pride" (*tuphōtheis*). This term is based upon the concept of smoke that comes from a smoldering fire (*tuphomai;* cf. Matt. 12:20). The imagery is that the influence of an exalted position can put such a

14. Found only here in the New Testament.

cloud of smoke around a person's spiritual eyes that he cannot see himself for what he really is. Elsewhere, the same word is seen as the adjectives "proud" (6:4) and "highminded" (II Tim. 3:4). Just as smoke rises rapidly only to lose its heat, so "pride gives a false sense of altitude."[15]

Second, the pastor could "fall into the condemnation of the devil." He will receive the same judgment (*krima*) Satan experienced.[16] When God originally created the angels, He assigned to Lucifer the position of hovering over the throne of God (Ezek. 28:14). Lucifer was thus marked by beauty, wisdom, brightness, and positional importance (Ezek. 28:17). He received this status immediately after his creation by God. He became so impressed with himself and his position that he subsequently, in his sin of pride, sought to be like God (Ezek. 28:15; Isa. 14:12–14). For this sin, he was removed from his position, became Satan, and was cast down in shame and embarrassment (Ezek. 28:17; Isa. 14:15–17). In like manner, the prestige of the pastoral office could so overwhelm a new convert that he could easily become proud and eventually fall from his spiritual leadership.

2. Good reputation (3:7)

The pastor must have "a good report of them which are without." The unsaved must bear witness (*marturian;* "report") that the qualities Paul listed are truly observable by them. The phrase "them which are without" (*tōn exōthen*) definitely refers to the unsaved who are outside of Christ "having no hope, and without God in the world" (Eph. 2:12; cf. I Cor. 5:12–13; Col. 4:5; I Thess. 4:12). The report comes from (*apo;* "of") them. What the candidate says about himself, what the church sees, and what the unsaved report should all agree.

Two problems will emerge if a person becomes a pastor apart from a good report from the lost. First, he could fall into "reproach" (*oneidismon*). Reproaches are verbal accusations hurled at another. They can be either justifiable criticism of wrongdoing (Matt. 11:20;

15. Guthrie, *The Pastoral Epistles,* p. 82.

16. Kent, *The Pastoral Epistles,* p. 135, and D. Edmond Hiebert, *First Timothy* (Chicago: Moody, 1957), p. 67.

Mark 16:14) or unjustifiable, hateful remarks spoken by enemies. In the latter sense, Jesus Christ was reproached or upbraided both during His life and at His death (Mark 15:32; Rom. 15:3). When believers live for Christ, they will suffer the same reproach (Matt. 5:11; I Peter 4:14). The problem addressed in this verse, however, is a justifiable criticism of the pastor's life by an unsaved man who knew something that the church did not.

Second, the pastor could fall into "the snare of the devil." Satan could use a fault, unknown to the saved but known to the lost, as a "snare" (*pagida*) or a trap in the future ministry of the pastor (6:9; II Tim. 2:26). A love of money could become that hidden snare (6:9).

As accurately as possible, the wise congregation must judge the qualifications of the candidate and try to ascertain whether he will act as consistently in the future as he has in the past. The church therefore should guard against hasty promotions of unproved candidates (cf. 5:22).

Questions for Discussion

1. What is proper preparation for the office of pastor? Is college necessary? seminary? internship?

2. How can a pastoral candidate determine whether his desire for that office is genuine? How can others detect that desire within him?

3. Do all sexual sins disqualify a pastoral candidate or a pastor? What about those committed before salvation?

4. How can the gift of teaching be detected? How can it be developed?

5. Since no believer is perfect, how can any candidate be blameless?

6. Should a pastor resign if his teen-age children become unruly? if they are addicted to drugs or in trouble with the law?

7. How long should a person be saved before he qualifies as a pastoral candidate? How can maturity be detected?

6

The Deacons and the Church

I Timothy 3:8–16

A local church consists of saints, bishops, and deacons (Phil. 1:1). The qualifications of the bishop have just been discussed (3:1–7). In this section, Paul set forth the requirements for the position of deacon (3:8–13) and the purpose of the entire church (3:14–16).

I. THE QUALIFICATIONS OF A DEACON (3:8–13)

The transitional conjunction "likewise" (*hōsautōs*) points back to the original verb "must be" (3:2). It is necessary for deacons to be possessors of basic qualities of spiritual leadership, just as the pastors are.

The "deacons" (*diakonous*) are those officers selected by the church to assist the bishop-pastor-elder. They should relieve the pastors of lesser responsibilities so that the pastors are able to devote more time and energy to prayer and to preaching (Acts 6:4). The office probably originated out of a need created by the rapid numerical growth of the church at Jerusalem (Acts 6:1–7). At that time, the Greeks murmured because some of their widows were being neglected in the daily ministration (*diakonia;* Acts 6:1). In recognition of the problem, the apostles exclaimed, "It is not reason that we should leave the word of God, and serve [*diakonein*] tables. Wherefore, brethren, look ye out among you seven men of honest report, full of the Holy Ghost and wisdom, whom we may appoint over this business" (Acts 6:2–3). Seven men were then selected. Although the official title *deacon* was not ascribed to them, two related words in the passage describe their responsibilities.

The qualifications for the office of deacon are high (Acts 6:3; I Tim. 3:8–13). When the apostolic era ended, the local churches had to use these guidelines to choose their deacons. Just as the first deacons relieved the apostles of mundane cares, so the deacons gradually relieved the pastor of those responsibilities that could be assumed by lay members.

The Greek word *diakonos* and its derivatives are used in a non-technical sense for a general ministry. Angels ministered to Christ at His temptation (Matt. 4:11), and they also serve believers (Heb. 1:14). Women ministered by giving financial assistance to the apostolic group (Mark 15:41). Preparing dinner was a ministry (Matt. 8:15). Christ ministred by giving His life on the cross (Matt. 20:28). Phebe was a female servant, a deaconess of the church at Cenchrea (Rom. 16:1). It is debatable whether she had an official position within the church or simply served in a general sense. Some scholars have suggested that the wives of the deacons served as deaconesses (3:11). Paul regarded himself and Apollos as ministers of the Word and of the church (I Cor. 3:5; Col. 1:23, 25).

The derivation of the word *deacon* is interesting. It is a compound word, based upon *dia* ("through") and *konis* ("dust"). The imagery suggests a man who moves quickly to perform his tasks and who creates a trail of dust by his haste. Deacons, therefore, must be dependable servants of the church and faithful assistants to the pastor.

A. Personal Qualifications (3:8–10)

These prerequisites are similar to those for the bishop. The fact that these church officers worked closely together would necessitate the sameness of moral background. Seven qualities are mentioned.

1. Grave

In the pagan world, the adjective "grave" (*semnous*) was applied to the gods. It also described their worshipers, who maintained a godlike majesty. Biblical usage, however, points to that which is ethically worthy of respect, stately, and dignified. A believer, in his conscious awareness of God, will manifest a seriousness of mind, character, and purpose. This word did not have the modern connotation of an austere or unbending spirit.

Gravity should mark all Christians (2:2; Phil. 4:8; Titus 2:2, 7) and especially the church officers (3:4, 8, 11).

2. Truthful

A deacon must not be "doubletongued." The term literally means "divided words" (*dilogous*).[1] He must be careful with his tongue, the most difficult member of the body to control (James 3:1–11). Since the deacon had close contact with both the bishop and the church members, he could not speak one thing to the pastor and the opposite to the people. He could not give two groups two different ideas about the same thing. He could not say one thing and mean something else. His yea must remain a yea and never be turned into a nay (II Cor. 1:18–19). He could not be a gossip.

3. Self-controlled

A deacon must not be "given to much wine." The verb (*prosechontas*) means "to hold toward," "to attach oneself to," or "to be addicted to." In this epistle, it is translated elsewhere as "giving heed" (1:4; 4:1) and "give attendance" (4:13). As the deacons went into the homes of believers, they would naturally be offered a drink of wine mixed with water. They could hardly refuse this expression of hospitality. In such situations, they must exercise self-control in the amount of their intake. They had to reject overindulgence.

4. Financially content

A deacon must not be "greedy of filthy lucre." This quality should also mark the bishop (3:3; Titus 1:7; I Peter 5:2). The compound term (*aischrokerdeis*) is made up of the word "gain" (*kerdos;* Phil. 1:21; 3:7) and the word "shame" (*aischron;* I Cor. 11:6; 14:35; Eph. 5:12). A deacon must not use his office for shameful

1. Used only here in the New Testament.

gain. The original deacons were involved in the distribution of goods and money to needy widows (Acts 6:1–7). Later in this epistle, Paul discussed the financial care of the widows, which was administered by the deacons (5:9, 16). In such a position of trust and confidence, it would be easy for a deacon to be tempted to steal from the church funds even as Judas Iscariot stole from the apostolic fund (John 12:6). The prior life of a candidate must exhibit a proper, biblical attitude toward money.

5. *Orthodox*

A deacon must be biblically sound in both belief and behavior. First, his doctrinal orthodoxy is described in the phrase "holding the mystery of the faith." The participle "holding" (*echontas*)[2] stresses constant, active steadfastness. He therefore must be committed to the fundamentals of the faith which he thoroughly understands. His defense of the truth, however, does not imply that he must also have the gift of teaching. The phrase "the mystery of the faith" is synonymous with the phrase "the mystery of godliness" (3:16). The word "mystery" (*mustērion*) is based on an ancient term that conveyed the idea of shutting the mouth.[3] The biblical use implies that "what was once silent is now vocal." Scriptural mysteries are divine truths unknown and unspoken by men in past ages, but now proclaimed and understood by yielded believers (I Cor. 2:7; 15:51). The mystery is the faith, the divinely revealed program of redemption centered in the death and resurrection of Jesus Christ and administered in this age through the church (Rom. 16:25–26; Eph. 3:9–11). Although a sinner must appropriate the benefits of redemption by individual faith, the phrase "the faith" (*tēs pisteōs*) points to the body of evangelical truth that forms the bedrock of orthodox Christianity. All believers must "contend for *the* faith which was once delivered unto the saints" (Jude 3; italics added).

Second, a deacon's moral orthodoxy is seen in the descriptive phrase "a pure conscience." A pure conscience is one that has been cleansed through regeneration and that remains clean by daily obedience to the word of Christ (John 13:10; 15:3). The adjectives *pure*

2. Present active participle.

3. This word is used twenty-seven times: three times in the Gospels; twenty times in Paul's letters; and four times in Revelation.

and *clean* are translations of the same term (*katharos*). The combination of a pure heart, a good conscience, and an unhypocritical faith will produce a pure conscience (1:5). The commitment of the deacons should follow the example of Timothy (1:19).

6. Proven

A deacon must be a tested, approved individual. The imperative ("let these also first be proved") shows that the entire church must apply certain qualifying tests to the candidate. He must be proved by others; he does not approve himself. The verb (*dokimazesthōsan*)[4] was used of assaying ore to prove the genuineness and quality of the precious metal. This moral and doctrinal observation was to be an ongoing process. An initial examination must be followed by subsequent scrutiny. Paul used the same concept in discussing the divine evaluation of his apostolic office: "But as we were allowed [same word; past tense] of God to be put in trust with the gospel, even so we speak; not as pleasing men, but God, which trieth [same word; present tense] our hearts" (I Thess. 2:4). The human and the divine examination of a candidate for the office of deacon should coincide.

The logical connective ("then") shows that approval precedes service. The lengthy phrase ("let them use the office of a deacon") is actually the translation of a single Greek word (*diakoneitōsan*).

7. Blameless

This adjective "blameless" (*anegklētoi*) is different from the other word also rendered as "blameless" (*anepilēmpton;* 3:2). It is a compound word that literally means "not called in." It is a legal term that is used elsewhere to describe the believer's justified position before God (I Cor. 1:8; Col. 1:22). No charge of condemnation can ever be brought against the believer in the court of divine justice. It is the answer to Paul's rhetorical question, "Who shall lay any thing to the charge [same word stem] of God's elect? It is God that justifieth" (Rom. 8:33).

In the same manner, both deacons and bishops must be blameless (3:10; Titus 1:6–7). In the courtroom of human evaluation, no proven

4. Present passive imperative.

charge of doctrinal or moral error should be laid against them. There naturally will be occasions when others disagree with them, but they must be innocent of all wrongdoing.

B. Family Qualifications (3:11–12)

There is some disagreement over the interpretation of the term "wives." The Greek word (*gunaikas*) can also be translated as "women." Two major views have emerged. First, some scholars believe that this verse gives the qualifications of a deaconess, a female church officer who is the counterpart of the male deacon.[5] Several arguments cited for this position include the identification of Phebe as "a servant [*diakonon*] of the church which is at Cenchrea" (Rom. 16:1); the use of the logical connective "even so" to introduce a new official group;[6] the lack of qualifications listed for the wife of the bishop; and no use of the possessive pronoun ("their").

The second interpretation views the women as the wives of the deacons. This seems to be the more plausible interpretation, for the following reasons. The discussion about the male deacon continues after this verse (3:12–13). If Paul introduced a new church office of deaconess, then he would have ended his list of qualifications for a deacon before that. It is possible that the pastor grew up within the church, served in various capacities (including the office of deacon), and eventually became the main administrative officer. Thus, the qualifications of a pastor's wife would have been seen earlier in his life. Paul could have created the feminine word *diakonē* for a distinctive female church officer. Phebe ministered to the church in a nontechnical sense (cf. Matt. 8:15; Mark 15:41).

The closeness of husband and wife would demand that both be godly and blameless in order to have an effective ministry. Since the office of deacon was created to meet a special need, then a local church has the autonomous right to create the position of deaconess to serve a distinctive purpose. The role of the woman in this office,

5. A. T. Robertson, *Word Pictures in the New Testament,* vol. 4 (Nashville: Broadman, 1931), p. 575, and Kenneth S. Wuest, *Word Studies in the Greek New Testament,* vol. 12, *The Pastoral Epistles* (Grand Rapids: Eerdmans, 1952), p. 61.

6. This Greek word *hōsautōs* is the same as that used in 3:8.

however, must not violate the principles of male headship discussed earlier in the epistle (2:11-15).

1. Godly wives (3:11)

Four virtues are mentioned. First, the wife must be "grave" (*semnas*). She must manifest a serious attitude in religious, family, and personal relationships. Such dignity and sobriety should mark all believers, including pastors and deacons (2:2; 3:4, 8). She must have control over her motivations.

Second, the wife must not be a slanderer, a person who harms others with malicious gossip. She must neither lie nor bear false witness. The term literally means "not an accuser," a person who casts a false charge through another. This word (*diabolous*), in the singular, always is translated as "the devil," a title for Satan (Matt. 4:1; Rev. 20:10). In the plural, it describes those who participate in character assassination (II Tim. 3:3; Titus 2:3). A deacon's wife must not be a "she-devil." She must have control over her tongue (Prov. 31:26).

Third, the wife must be "sober" (*nēphalious*). She must be spiritually alert and sensitive to the inroads of moral and doctrinal error (cf. 3:2; Titus 2:2). The term does not apply to the subject of drinking alcoholic beverages.

Fourth, the wife must be "faithful in all things." She must be dependable and trustworthy. Her husband, children, and church can count on her to do what she promised.

2. Marital fidelity (3:12a)

Deacons must be "the husbands of one wife." Literally, the phrase reads "one-woman men" (*mias gunaikos andres*). They have the same marital qualifications as the pastor does (3:2). They must have only one living wife; thus, they cannot be divorced and remarried.

3. Family ruler (3:12b)

In his family leadership, a deacon must exercise the same control as the pastor does (3:4). He must "rule" or "stand before" (*proistamenoi*) his children and his house well. The latter designation includes slaves and other family members. As he administers the affairs of the home, he must deserve the respect of his family. The adverb "well" (*kalōs*) stresses observable spiritual goodness that is beautiful to the witness.

C. Responsibility (3:13)

In his conclusion to this section, Paul mentioned two rewards that would come to the deacon for excellent service.

1. Performance of the task

The opening phrase literally reads, "For the ones who have deaconed well. . . ." Earlier Paul stressed the daily function of the deacon, but here he points to the completion of the task, from start to finish.[7] The length of service for the deacon is not stated in the Scriptures. Since deacons were appointed to meet a particular need, their office could terminate when the need no longer existed. There is no indication whether they were elected to a lifetime office or simply to a limited term, subject to later renewal. Again, the local church has the prerogative to define the conditions and length of the deacons' ministry.

2. Promise of reward

A deacon who serves well[8] is promised two rewards. The verb "purchase" (*peripoiountai*) means "to acquire" or "to obtain." It does not connote the use of money. The same verb and its cognate noun are used to describe the purchased possession of believing sinners by the redemptive work of Christ (Acts 20:28; Eph. 1:14; I Thess. 5:9; II Thess. 2:14; Heb. 10:39; I Peter 2:9). God always rewards faithful service, both in this life and in the future world (Matt. 25:23). The first reward is a "good degree" (*bathmon kalon*).[9] This unique term refers to the steps of a door's threshold or to the steps of a stairway (I Sam. 5:5). It conveys the idea of a place to stand

7. The first verb is in the present tense (3:10), but this second verb is in the aorist tense (3:13).

8. The adverb "well" definitely goes with the first verb, not with the second ("purchase").

9. The term *bathmon* is found only here in the New Testament.

with a view to ascend higher. In the spiritual sense, it points to an acceptable standing before God and His people. The passage may point to a position of importance that will be given to the faithful deacon at the judgment seat of Christ and that will be exercised in the millennial kingdom. It is plausible that a proven deacon may be selected by a church to serve as its elder. Following that interpretation, a person could use the office of deacon as a step of promotion to the office of pastor. Several of the church fathers, in their writings, suggest this possibility.

The second reward is "great boldness in the faith which is in Christ Jesus." The term "boldness" (*parrēsian*) stresses a freedom of speech. Believers will respect and heed the spoken counsel of a dedicated deacon. Faithful service will open up opportunities of direction and teaching within the realm of evangelical truth. It is possible that the boldness of speech might be that which is manifested in the day of judgment by a deacon who has nothing to hide or to fear (I John 4:17). It could also point to a believing confidence in prayer that is supported by a blameless life.

II. THE CHURCH

Paul hoped to rejoin Timothy in Ephesus after the former's ministry in Macedonia terminated (1:3). In fact, his return was imminent ("shortly"). The apostle, however, recognized the possibility of a delay ("But if I tarry long"); therefore, he wanted to write to Timothy about his plans and the associate's responsibilities (3:14–15a).

A. Nature of the Church (3:15)

Belonging to God presupposes appropriate behavior. The purpose of the letter is indicated by the conjunction "that" (*hina*). Paul wrote, ". . . that thou mayest know how *thou* oughtest to behave *thyself*" (italics added). The two italicized pronouns actually do not appear in the Greek text.[10] It is possible to insert such words as

10. *Hina eidēis pōs dei in oikōi theou anastrephesthai.*

"men" and "themselves" to make the sentence read, ". . . that thou mayest know how men ought to behave themselves." Regardless, the guidelines of behavior pertain to both the administrative leader and the people.

The sphere of spiritual behavior is "in" the church. In this verse, the church is described in three ways.

1. The house of God

The church is the "house of God" (*oikōi theou*).[11] This title emphasizes the place where God dwells. In the Old Testament, God visibly manifested His presence to Israel by dwelling within the tabernacle Moses constructed and the temple Solomon built (II Chron. 7:1–3; Mark 2:26). God, however, was not limited to these places, which were subject to decay and destruction. Since He is omnipresent, He can be present everywhere in the totality of His being (I Kings 8:27).

In the gospel era, Jesus identified the second temple, which had been defiled by the religious establishment (John 2:16), as the house of God the Father.

In this age, however, God manifests His indwelling presence in redeemed people. The body of each believer serves as the temple of God (I Cor. 6:19–20). Corporately, believing members of a local church constitute the sanctuary of God (I Cor. 3:16–17). Christians are being built as a "spiritual house" (I Peter 2:5). As "the house of God," His judgment will fall on them before it descends upon the unsaved (I Peter 4:17).

2. The church of the living God

The church is also "the church of the living God." The term "church" (*ekklēsia*) literally means "a called-out group." The word is used in four different ways in the New Testament. First, it referred to a secular assembly, the freemen of Ephesus, gathered together for civil business (Acts 19:32, 39, 41). Second, Stephen equated Israel in her wilderness wanderings with a church (Acts 7:38). Third, the local church was a group of believers meeting in a specific locality,

11. No definite article appears before the noun.

organized under the leadership of pastors and deacons, to perpetuate the ordinances of baptism and the Lord's Supper and to propagate the gospel (Rom. 16:5). Fourth, the universal church includes all believers from the descent of the Holy Spirit on the day of Pentecost to the return of Christ for His own (Eph. 1:22–23).

Christ predicted that He would build His church upon His redemptive death and resurrection (Matt. 16:18–21).[12] His church is also equated with His body, the spiritual union of Christ and believers (Eph. 1:22–23). At His ascension into heaven, He became the living head of His body-church. At regeneration, believing sinners are baptized in the Holy Spirit into a positional oneness both in Christ and within the universal church (I Cor. 12:13).

The universal church finds its living application in local congregations of believers who gather together for mutual worship, instruction, and evangelization. Proper behavior in the church thus constitutes godly living within the local assembly and through contact with other believers from different geographical locations. In the apostolic era, there were no believers who functioned outside of the organization of local churches (Acts 2:41–47; 14:23).

The "church of the living God" includes both the universal church and the local church. In contrast to the Ephesian temples dedicated to nonexistent deities, living believers have been called out of the world of lost humanity by the one and only living God.

3. *The pillar and ground of the truth*

The church did not originate redemptive truth, but she must sustain it. Actually, the truth, centered in Christ's person and work, gave birth to the church (John 14:6).

The two architectural metaphors show the relationship of the church to the truth. First, the church is a "pillar" (*stulos*). The temple of Diana in Ephesus had 127 pillars, which supported the roof. The church of living believers, in its corporate oneness, is to hold up the truth in its own generation. The genuine believer-overcomer is promised that he will be a pillar in the eternal temple of God (Rev. 3:12).

12. Since the church of Christ is the church of God, then Christ must also be God.

Second, the church is a "ground" (*hedraiōma*).[13] This term, which means "a firm foundation," is related to the adjective "stedfast" (I Cor. 7:37; 15:58; Col. 1:23). The church, in its dual ecclesiastical function, must be both the protector and the propagator of truth.

B. Nature of the Truth (3:16)

The phrase "without controversy" literally means "confessedly." The term (*homologoumenōs*) is based upon a verb that means "to say the same thing as."[14] The word denotes common consent. All believers, members of the church, must openly acknowledge these redemptive truths as they serve together as "the pillar and ground of the truth."

Church members affirm that "great is the mystery of godliness." The mystery centers in Christ and His relationship to His people (Eph. 5:30, 32). This mystery involves a recognition that God the Son became man and that the divine-human Christ died and rose again. It acknowledges subjectively a oneness with Christ through positional identification with Him by repentant faith and regeneration. In this age, Christ cannot be separated from His people (Acts 9:4; Gal. 1:13).

Six affirmations of doctrinal truth are stated.

1. God was manifest in the flesh[15]

John F. Walvoord writes, "The incarnation of the Lord Jesus Christ is the central fact of Christianity. Upon it the whole superstructure of Christian theology depends."[16] God the Son, an eternal person within the trinitarian oneness of the divine Being, took to Himself a perfect and complete human nature through the virgin conception and birth. He, who was spirit in essence, "was made flesh" (John 1:14; 4:24). As a consequence, He is today one person

13. Used only here in the New Testament.

14. Used only here in the New Testament. The verb normally translates as "confess" (I John 1:9).

15. The critical Greek text has the relative pronoun *hos* ("he who") rather than *theos* ("God").

16. *Jesus Christ Our Lord* (Chicago: Moody, 1974), p. 96.

with two natures, divine and human.[17] A denial of the incarnation reveals the spirit of antichrist (I John 4:1–3).

2. Justified in the Spirit

This phrase could refer either to the anointing of Christ by the Holy Spirit at the baptism or to the resurrection of Christ. Throughout His earthly ministry, Jesus preached and performed miracles under the enablement of the Spirit (Isa. 61:1; Luke 4:18–21; Acts 10:38). At His crucifixion, He offered Himself to God as a sacrifice through the eternal Spirit (Heb. 9:14). In His resurrection, He was quickened by the Spirit (Rom. 8:11; I Peter 3:18).

3. Seen of angels

Angels were actively involved in the life and ministry of Jesus Christ. Gabriel announced to Mary that she would be the mother of the Messiah (Luke 1:26–38). Angels proclaimed His birth to the shepherds (Luke 2:8–14), ministered to Christ after His temptation (Matt. 4:11), strengthened Him when He earnestly prayed in Gethsemane (Luke 22:43), declared His resurrection to the women (Luke 24:4–7), and explained His ascension to the apostles (Acts 1:10–11). Angels have learned about divine wisdom and grace as they have observed the redemptive program in operation through the church (Eph. 3:10; I Peter 1:12). The primary emphasis of the phrase in this verse is probably upon the empirical perception of Christ's resurrection and ascension.

4. Preached unto the Gentiles

The gospel of Christ's redemptive death and resurrection was proclaimed to the Gentiles by Paul (Eph. 3:1–12). The gospel's mysterious character is seen in the fact that believing Gentiles would become fellow members with saved Jews in the true church (Eph. 3:6). Both Jews and Gentiles were saved in the old dispensation, but they remained ethnically and positionally distinct. In Christ, however, there is neither Jew nor Gentile (Gal. 3:28).

17. Theologians call this truth the hypostatic union. For more information, consult Robert Gromacki, *The Virgin Birth: Doctrine of Deity* (Grand Rapids: Baker, 1974).

5. *Believed on in the world*

The gospel of the grace of God is "the power of God unto salvation to every one that believeth; to the Jew first, and also to the Greek" (Rom. 1:16). Proclamation brought response. The provision of salvation had to be appropriated by faith alone, apart from any human effort.

6. *Received up into glory*

The ascension of the resurrected Christ into heaven occurred fifty days after His death and resurrection (Acts 1:2, 11, 22). His ascension manifested that His sacrificial work had been accomplished (Heb. 1:3). His ascension established Him as the exalted head of the church that He began to build (Eph. 1:20–23). The next event in the mystery is the return of Christ to take resurrected Christians and living believers into His presence (I Cor. 15:51–53).

Questions for Discussion

1. What should a church do if no men meet the qualifications for the office of deacon? Should the standards be changed?
2. If a deacon fails after he has been appointed, should he be removed? How?
3. Should candidates for the office of deacon be given an oral or written doctrinal examination? What basic doctrines should these candidates understand?
4. How can the wives of deacons, or deaconesses, be used effectively within a local church?
5. How can a local church protect the truth of evangelical Christianity? How can they propagate it?
6. Is denominationalism correct? How can it fit in with the truth of the universal church?
7. Do Christians understand the concept of the incarnation of Christ? of the Trinity?

7

The Peril of Apostasy

I Timothy 4:1–5

In the first three chapters of this epistle, Paul charged Timothy to confront the legalists (1) and instructed him about proper conduct of the local church with respect to prayer, women, pastors, and deacons (2–3). In the last half of the epistle, the apostle gave his associate counsel about numerous issues that affected Timothy's personal conduct and ministry. These topics include apostasy (4:1–5), the nature of the ministry (4:6–16), members of the church (5:1–2), the care of widows (5:3–16), elders (5:17–25), slaves (6:1–2), greedy teachers (6:3–10), Timothy's own integrity (6:11–16), wealthy believers (6:17–19), and false science (6:20–21).

I. THE WARNING AGAINST APOSTASY (4:1–3a)

The connective "now" (*de*) shows the transition from the confession of redemptive truth by the true church (3:15–16) to the repudiation of orthodoxy by the apostate church. In most of his epistles, Paul had to deal with the problems of moral and doctrinal apostasy (Rom. 16:17–18; I Cor. 15:12; II Cor. 11:1–4, 13–15; Gal. 1:6–9; Phil. 3:2, 17–19; Col. 2:4–19; II Thess. 2:1–3; II Tim. 3:1–5; Titus 1:9–16). Such error must be detected early and refuted by informed leaders of local churches.

A. Prediction about Apostasy (4:1a)

When Jesus Christ spoke about the signs that would precede His second advent, He predicted the rise of false Christs and false prophets (Matt. 24:4–5, 11). In this passage, Paul further delineated the error those false teachers would expound.

1. The prophecy was given by the Holy Spirit

All Scripture has been breathed out by God; it is divinely inspired (II Tim. 3:16). It did not originate within the thought processes of man; rather, "holy men of God spake as they were moved by the Holy Ghost" (II Peter 1:21). All biblical authors acknowledged that God worked in and through them to communicate His word in both spoken and written form. When they were under this divine control, they spoke and wrote exactly what God wanted to say. They neither added nor subtracted anything. The result was the inscripturated, inerrant, infallible Word of God, the only basis of faith and practice. In essence, what authenticated prophets and apostles wrote was what God wrote. Such phrases as "Paul says," "the Bible says," and "God says" are synonymous. The Bible, therefore, is a divine-human book.

The Holy Spirit is the key personal agent in divine revelation, inspiration, and illumination (I Cor. 2:10–13). Paul thus wrote, "Which things also we speak, not in the words which man's wisdom teacheth, but which the Holy Ghost teacheth" (I Cor. 2:13). Peter acknowledged that the Spirit spoke by the mouth of David (Acts 1:16) and Paul confessed that the Spirit spoke by Isaiah (Acts 28:25). What the Spirit spoke was what those respective men wrote.

The use of the present tense "speaketh" (*legei*) shows that the Spirit was carrying on a continuous ministry of warning through the apostles. Both before and after the writing of I Timothy, Paul and the other apostles constantly admonished the church to watch out for the apostates (II Tim. 3:1; II Peter 2:1; 3:3; I John 2:18–19; 4:1–3; II John 7–11; Jude 3–4, 17–19). In this passage, Paul is specifically attributing this written warning to the oracular influence of the Holy Spirit.

The adverb "expressly" (*rhētōs*) denotes that which is articulated explicitly and distinctly.[1] It is derived from the verb "to speak" (*rheō*), a verb that is often used to refer to written revelation spoken

1. Used only here in the New Testament.

by God (Matt. 1:22; 2:15; Rom. 9:12). Thus, no human speculation was involved in this prophecy.

2. The prophecy referred to the latter times

The "mystery of iniquity," which would reach its acme in the manifestation of the man of sin, was already working in the lifetime of Paul (II Thess. 2:7). John declared that the spirit of antichrist, embodied in many antichrists, was already in the world (I John 2:18–19; 4:1–3). Paul had previously announced to the Ephesian elders that false teachers would immediately arise after his departure from their city (Acts 20:29–31).

The phrase "latter times" (*husterois kairois*), however, refers to the latter days of the apostolic era. Later, Peter likewise predicted the infiltration of false teachers (II Peter 2:1); subsequently, Jude declared that they had already arrived (Jude 4). In a more general sense, the phrase describes the closing years of the church age. Donald Guthrie comments that it is "a phrase which suggests a more imminent future than 'in the last days' (used in 2 Tim. 3:1)."[2]

The plural "times" rather than the singular "time" points to "the critical, epoch-making periods of time foreordained of God."[3] It does not refer to mere time (*chronos*) indicated by the calendar, but to those future developments over which God has sovereign control and through which God will accomplish His ultimate purpose. The phrase ("latter times") must also be contrasted with the "last days" of divine revelation (Heb. 1:2) and the last days of God's program for Israel (Joel 2:28–32; Acts 1:6–7). These phrases are not synonymous; rather, each use must be viewed in its own context.

3. The prophecy described the apostasy

Three facts must be included in a proper definition of the apostasy. First, this apostasy involves people. The indefinite pronoun "some" (*tines*) probably includes both the false teachers and

2. *The Pastoral Epistles,* Tyndale Bible Commentary (Grand Rapids: Eerdmans, 1972), p. 91.

3. Kenneth S. Wuest, *Word Studies in the Greek New Testament,* vol. 12, *The Pastoral Epistles* (Grand Rapids: Eerdmans, 1952), p. 66.

their converts.[4] There is no indication that the pronoun implies a majority or a sizable minority.

Second, the apostasy involves willful departure. The verb "shall depart" (*apostēsontai*) can be transliterated as "apostasize." Literally the verb means "to stand away from" (*apo* and *histēmi*). In a non-technical sense, the word simply means a physical removal from one place to another (Luke 2:37; 4:13; Acts 12:10). In an ecclesiastical sense, apostasy occurs when people depart from the fundamentals of orthodox theology and take a stance outside of that realm. D. Edmond Hiebert correctly observes that "an apostate is not one who gives up his profession of being a Christian, but one who forsakes the truth of the Christian faith."[5]

Third, the apostasy is a departure from "the faith" (*tēs pisteōs*). The presence of the definite article shows that apostasy is a defection from the body of doctrinal truth that one must accept in order to become a Christian. It is "*the* faith which was once delivered unto the saints" (Jude 3, italics added). The faith embraces the eternal deity of Jesus Christ, His incarnation through the virgin conception and birth, His sinless life, His substitutionary, atoning death on the cross, His bodily resurrection and ascension, and His physical return. It also involves the truth that a man is justified by faith in Christ alone, apart from any meritorious work practiced either before or after regeneration. Apostasy, therefore, is a radical departure from the evangelical faith. The departure does not issue in a loss of personal salvation; rather, it results in the façade of a faulty profession. An apostate thus is an unsaved person who eventually reveals his true spiritual identity by his voluntary denial of redemptive truth. John correctly analyzed the apostates: "They went out from us, but they were not of us: for if they had been of us, they would no doubt have continued with us: but they went out, that they might be made manifest that they were not all of us" (I John 2:19).

B. Description of the Apostasy (4:1b–3a)

The first three verses constitute one complete sentence with some complex grammatical structure. Only one verb form ("giving heed")

4. Some scholars limit the meaning to the misled followers. Wuest, *ibid.*
5. *First Timothy* (Chicago: Moody, 1957), p. 76.

actually refers to the pronoun "some." The other English verb forms ("speaking," "having," and "forbidding") appear to refer to the same pronoun, but they do not. They all, however, describe the marks of apostasy.

1. Seducing spirits

Apostates are marked by "giving heed to seducing spirits." The participle (*prosechontes*),[6] discussed earlier (3:8), means "to give assent, to take to one's possession." They willingly accept error; thus they are morally culpable.

The "seducing spirits" (plural) must be contrasted with the Spirit (singular). Redemptive truth is singular; there is only "one faith" (Eph. 4:5). The Holy Spirit communicated that oneness of truth through forty human authors of the sixty-six inspired books. All of the prophets and apostles complemented each other in the exposition of the divine plan for redemption. On the other hand, apostasy takes many forms because it originates with multiple spirits. Just as the Holy Spirit spoke through holy men of God, so evil spirits communicate through evil men. False prophets thus are supernaturally controlled by seducing spirits, who are fallen angels or unclean demons within the realm of Satan.

John cautioned, "Beloved, believe not every spirit, but try the spirits whether they are of God: because many false prophets are gone out into the world" (I John 4:1). The spirits are examined by a thorough evaluation of the doctrines of cults, with special attention to their approach to the person and redemptive work of Jesus Christ (I John 4:6).

These spirits are "seducing" (*planois*)[7] in that they cause people to wander from the truth. They deceive and lead astray.

2. Doctrines of demons

Apostates also give heed to doctrines of demons. The term "devils" should be translated as "demons" (*daimoniōn*). There is only one devil, Satan, but there are many demons or fallen angelic

6. Present active participle, nominative, masculine, plural, in grammatical agreement with *tines* ("some").

7. The English term *planet* is based upon this word.

spirits who comprise his hierarchy of evil (Eph. 6:12). Demonic wisdom, manifested in apostate teaching, includes self-glorification, lying, humanism, and sensuality (James 3:14–16). Such error has been formulated into various doctrinal systems. It is organized and attractive to man's natural instincts, but it is "damnable" heresy (II Peter 2:1). Both the advocates and converts of apostate doctrines are thoroughly blinded by Satan (II Cor. 4:3–4).

3. *Lies and hypocrisy*

The passage literally reads, ". . . giving heed to seducing spirits, and doctrines of demons in hypocrisy of liars" (*en hupokrisei pseudologōn*).[8] It is not that some apostates or demons are speaking lies in hypocrisy; rather, the means of deceptive doctrine is in the realm of hypocrisy put forth by lying men. Apostasy often masquerades as holy, righteous living within a caring community. It is hypocritical in that it shows an external form of religious goodness, but its essence is error declared by teachers who deliberately misrepresent evangelical truth, which they aggressively repudiate. Such men are "false apostles, deceitful workers, transforming themselves into the apostles of Christ" (II Cor. 11:13). Just as an unholy Satan changes himself into an angel of light, so his human ministers are transformed into the "ministers of righteousness" (II Cor. 11:14–15). The original temptation of Adam and Eve was effected by Satan in the realm of lying hypocrisy (II Cor. 11:3–4).

4. *Seared conscience*

These lying hypocrites, the human agents who are energized by demons, have literally "cauterized their own conscience" (*kekautēriasmenōn tēn idian suneidēsin*). The prepositional phrase ("with a hot iron") was added to make the imagery especially vivid. Hiebert states that the expression was "derived from the penal practice of branding certain criminals on their forehead."[9]

All men have a conscience, but in their sinful lives, they rationalize their behavior, blame it on someone else, or point to another

8. The term *pseudologōn* only occurs here in the New Testament.
9. *First Timothy,* p. 77.

who is worse (Rom. 2:15). Isaiah cried, "Woe unto them that call evil good, and good evil" (Isa. 5:20). The tense of this participle shows that there was a time when these people openly rejected truth and embraced error and that their present apostate condition could be traced to that event.[10] Homer A. Kent, Jr., remarks that they were "made insensitive to right and wrong because of some radical act of perverting the truth."[11] As Paul observed, they "being past feeling have given themselves over unto lasciviousness, to work all uncleanness with greediness" (Eph. 4:19).

5. Celibacy

The phrase "forbidding to marry" again refers to the hypocritical liars, the apostate teachers who are demonically controlled.[12] Their prohibition of marriage reveals an asceticism that rejects the divine ordinance of marriage established in the Garden of Eden, sanctioned by Jesus Christ, and approved by the apostles (Gen. 2:18–25; Matt. 19:3–12; I Cor. 7:2–7). The apostates decreed that no marriage was preferable to the abuses of marriage. They saw in celibacy the ultimate expression of total devotion to God. The starvation of divinely given sexual drives, however, is not the biblical way to avoid sexual sins. Selfless love between husband and wife truly honors God and illustrates the spiritual union between Christ and His church (Eph. 5:22–33).

6. Asceticism

Another mark of this apostasy was "to abstain from meats." The term "meats" (*brōmatōn*) includes both meat and vegetables. The restriction of diet, through a list of forbidden foods or enforced fasting, manifests a legalism that is hostile to the principles of grace. Early man was vegetarian (Gen. 1:29), but after the flood,

10. It is a perfect middle participle, deponent: *kekautēriasmenōn*. It is in the genitive case, agreeing with the noun "liars" (*pseudologōn*).

11. *The Pastoral Epistles* (Chicago: Moody, 1979), p. 151.

12. The participle *kōluontōn* ("forbidding") is in the genitive case, agreeing with the noun "liars."

God enlarged the human diet to include meat (Gen. 9:3). The Mosaic law limited the intake of meat to prescribed types (Lev. 11). A distinction was made between clean and unclean beasts. Since a Christian is not under any obligation to the Mosaic law, he is free to enjoy all types of food provided by his bountiful Father (Acts 10:9–16; I Cor. 10:26).

Asceticism and legalism are two means that false teachers use to control totally the lives of their disciples. Paul warned all believers, "Let no man therefore judge you in meat, or in drink" (Col. 2:16). Later in this epistle, the apostle declared that God richly gives His own "all things to enjoy" (6:17). Ascetics, however, see sin in the proper enjoyment of divine provision for the needs of the body.

II. THE IGNORANCE OF APOSTASY

Apostates usually claim to know something that no one has ever thought of before. Paul warned against such egotistical speculation: "Beware lest any man spoil you through philosophy and vain deceit, after the tradition of men, after the rudiments of the world, and not after Christ" (Col. 2:8).

Such arrogant teachers are actually ignorant of God's revealed purposes. Two examples are given.

A. Purpose of Creation (4:3b)

The relative pronoun "which" (*ha*) definitely refers to the solid foods ("meats"), but it could also include the institution of marriage.[13] The purposes of both originated within the Garden of Eden.

1. Meats should be received

God created food "to be received" (*eis metalēpsin*).[14] This word connotes participation and thus, in the context of this verse, eating.

13. The second view is held by Kent, *The Pastoral Epistles,* p. 153, and Hiebert, *First Timothy,* p. 78.

14. Used only here in the New Testament.

The verb form on which the word is based is used of the believers in the church at Jerusalem who "did eat their meat with gladness and singleness of heart" (Acts 2:46), of the passengers on the ship who were encouraged by Paul "to take some meat" (Acts 27:34), and of the husbandman who is a "partaker of the fruits" (II Tim. 2:6).

God said to Adam, "Behold, I have given you every herb bearing seed, which is upon the face of all the earth, and every tree, in the which is the fruit of a tree yielding seed; to you it shall be for meat" (Gen. 1:29). Even the animals could enjoy the vegetation for their nourishment (Gen. 1:30). After the flood in Noah's day, God increased the scope of man's diet to include the animals that He sustained through the deluge (Gen. 9:3).

Such bounty was to be received "with thanksgiving." A grateful heart will always express itself through spoken praise to the Giver of all good things. Reception without thanksgiving is impudence. One characteristic of the perilous times in the last days is an unthankful spirit (II Tim. 3:2). Solomon correctly observed that "the plowing of the wicked, is sin" (Prov. 21:4). The creation of food supplies that renew themselves from generation to generation was designed to bring glory to God. Foods reveal His power, goodness, and loving concern for human life. When men see only food per se, and not food as divine provision, then the seed of incipient apostasy has already begun to sprout within them.

2. Meats should be received by believers

Those who belong to God should instinctively receive divinely given meats with thanksgiving. These people are described in two ways.[15] First, they are believers. They initially believed in Christ for salvation and continue to trust in Him.

Second, these believers "know the truth." The perfect tense of the participle (*epegnōkosi*) points to a past time when they came to know God through the redemptive truth of the gospel message. Knowing the truth is synonymous with knowing God and Christ. Jesus Himself said, "And this is life eternal, that they might know thee the only true God, and Jesus Christ, whom thou hast sent"

15. They are one group with two characteristics. The Granville Sharp rule operates here: one article appears with two verbal adjectives.

(John 17:3). Salvation thus is knowing God redemptively and being known by Him (Gal. 4:9).

The verb means that a person has thorough, personal knowledge.[16] It is a knowledge that leads to commitment of life with full confidence and trust in the object of that faith.

B. Nature of Creation (4:4–5)

The conjunction "for" (*hoti*) introduced a second point about the apostates' ignorance. The apostates failed to comprehend the essence of the created thing. Four assertions are made by the apostle.

1. Every created food is good

The work of creation ended with this assessment: "And God saw every thing that he had made, and, behold, it was very good" (Gen. 1:31). Only good things can come from a good and perfect God (James 1:17). Things are good not only because He made them, but also because they are totally suited to meet the needs of man's physical sustenance in this world. God designed "meats for the belly, and the belly for meats" (I Cor. 6:13). The two are compatible and necessary until man receives his immortal, incorruptible body, which will function in the eternal state.

2. No created food should be refused

Created food was designed for consumption, not for rejection. The verbal adjective "to be refused" means "to cast away from."[17] The basic verb was used of blind Bartimaeus, who cast away his garment when he met Jesus (Mark 10:50), and of believers, who should not cast away their confidence in God (Heb. 10:35). When some food is placed before these apostates, they push it away and declare it to be taboo.

3. Created food should be received with thanksgiving

When Jesus multiplied the bread and fish in order to feed the multitudes, He gave thanks for the provision (Matt. 14:19; 15:36).

16. Note the *epi* prefix to the verb.
17. Used only here in the New Testament.

When He instituted the ordinance of the Lord's Supper, He thanked God for the elements, which represented His body and blood (I Cor. 11:24). If the incarnate Son of God was thankful, then His followers should also express their gratitude.

4. Created food should be sanctified

Within the Mosaic economy for Israel, many things were sanctified or set apart for sacred use: places, garments, vessels, and sacrificial food. In the New Testament era, the child of God must view all activity with a sacred perception; thus Paul wrote, "Whether therefore ye eat, or drink, or whatsoever ye do, do all to the glory of God" (I Cor. 10:31). Spirituality is not determined by a restricted, legalistic diet (Rom. 14:17), but it is manifested through a biblical use of divinely created food.

The conjunction "for" (*gar*) explains why believers can receive all food with thanksgiving. The verb ("it is sanctified") can be translated "it is being sanctified" (*hagiazetai*).[18] Whenever food is eaten, believers can actively set it apart for its divine purpose in their lives.

Two means of sanctification are given. Both are operative at the same time.[19] First, the "word of God" is the teaching of Scripture about food: its source, essence, and purpose. The Bible alone must remain the basis of faith and practice. The opinions of cultists, legalists, and nutritionists should never be superimposed upon the inscripturated Word of God.

Second, in his "prayer" the believer must thank God for His provision and request that the divine purpose for the food be carried out within the lives of the partakers. The people of Israel would not eat until Samuel had blessed the sacrifice (I Sam. 9:13). After Paul had given thanks for food in the presence of his travel companions, he began to eat (Acts 27:35). The multitudes did not eat until Jesus had blessed the bread and the fish (Matt. 14:19; 15:36).

Questions for Discussion

1. How would you respond to a person who claimed that God the Holy Spirit had spoken to him directly and audibly? How does God speak today?

18. Present passive indicative.
19. There is one preposition with two subjects: *dia logou theou kai enteuxeōs.*

2. What contemporary religious movements are apostate? How did these movements start? What basic truths do they deny?

3. What seducing and lying means do cults use to gain converts? How can people be warned against these cults?

4. How trustworthy is the conscience? in an unsaved person? in a believer?

5. What contemporary groups practice celibacy and asceticism? Why are people attracted to such groups?

6. How should the Christian respond to people who recommend the elimination of certain foods, such as sugar or red meat, from the diet?

7. Should believers thank God for their food at every meal? in private? in public?

8

The Impact of a Biblical Ministry

I Timothy 4:6–16

Coaches excite their players, generals motivate their armies, and teachers influence their students. In the arena of religion, the same situation prevails. Devotees usually follow a charismatic preacher rather than an ethical principle. The impact of an authoritative, dominant personality on crowds is an observable fact.

Paul encourged others to follow him as he was following Christ (I Cor. 11:1). He wanted Timothy to provide a role model of the biblical minister to the Ephesian church in contrast to the hypocritical apostates. In this section of the epistle, Paul charged his younger associate to manifest the truth of God in his teaching and lifestyle.

I. THE MARKS OF A GOOD MINISTER (4:6–8)

The future declaration ("thou shalt be a good minister of Jesus Christ") does not imply that Timothy was a bad leader at the time the letter was written. Rather, Paul told Timothy how he could continue to be a good minister in the midst of a difficult situation at Ephesus.

A. Biblical Exposition (4:6a)

The apostle wanted Timothy to "put the brethren in remembrance of these things." His primary ministry was to the saved, not to the apostates. A faithful shepherd must protect and feed the sheep. Hunting wolves is not a substitute for caring for the flock.

Timothy, however, had to inform the church about the erroneous concepts of the apostates. The phrase "these things" definitely includes the content of the preceding section (4:1–5).[1] Paul likewise constantly warned his readers against the inroads of wolves in sheep's clothing (Acts 20:29; Phil. 3:2).

The verbal participle (*hupotithemenos*) literally means "to put under."[2] It is used only once elsewhere—of Aquila and Priscilla, who "laid down their own necks" for Paul (Rom. 16:4). Timothy had a solemn responsibility to place this divinely revealed repudiation of apostasy before the church for its microscopic scrutiny. He had to place doctrinal steppingstones under the Ephesians' feet so they would not slip and fall into apostasy.

B. Maturity (4:6b)

The best defense against error is the offense of personal growth toward maturity. In the performance of his task, Timothy could not neglect his own spiritual nourishment. The verb (*entrephomenos*)[3] stresses a constant, internal feeding and strengthening process. Two means of sustenance are set forth.

1. Words of the faith

The fundamentals of redemptive, evangelical theology are meant by the phrase "the words of faith" (*tois logois tēs pisteōs*). This literally is "*the* faith," the same faith that deacons must hold and that apostates have repudiated (3:9; 4:1). It is not personal faith that increases through the hearing of the revealed Word (Mark 9:24; Rom. 10:17). The use of the plural ("the words") points to the multiple prophetic and apostolic pronouncements, both spoken and written. Together, and later as the inscripturated text took form, they became the basis of faith and practice.

1. The phrase "these things" (*tauta*) is emphasized; it appears first in the sentence.
2. The KJV regards it as a conditional participle with the resultant "if" translation.
3. Present participle, deponent. Used only here in the New Testament.

2. Words of good doctrine

The former phrase dealt with revelation, whereas this one focuses on instruction. Timothy had been taught well: first by his mother and grandmother (II Tim. 1:5); then by the leaders at Lystra (Acts 16:1–2); and finally by Paul (II Tim. 2:2). The apostle later encouraged his associate, "But continue thou in the things which thou hast learned and hast been assured of, knowing of whom thou hast learned them" (II Tim. 3:14).

The relative clause ("whereunto thou hast attained") refers to the doctrine.[4] The verb (*parēkolouthēkas*) literally means "to follow beside." At some point in his life, Timothy closely investigated what he had been taught, accepted it wholeheartedly, and continued in that theological conviction.[5] Luke used this same verb when he exclaimed that he "had perfect understanding" of all things pertaining to Christ's virgin birth and genealogy (Luke 1:3). Subsequently, Paul wrote to Timothy, "But thou hast fully known [same verb] my doctrine, manner of life, purpose, faith, longsuffering, charity, patience" (II Tim. 3:10). Timothy apparently checked Paul very carefully before he became a staunch follower of the apostle.

C. Godliness (4:7–8)

The term "godliness" (*eusebeia*) occurs eight times in this epistle (2:2; 3:16; 4:7, 8; 6:3, 5, 6, 11), and only seven times elsewhere (Acts 3:12; II Tim. 3:5; Titus 1:1; II Peter 1:3, 6, 7; 3:11). It is never used as an attribute of deity; rather, it is descriptive of believers, with two possible exceptions (Acts 10:2, 7; 22:12). The term stresses outward piety and reverent respect of God and holy things.

1. Godliness involves denial (4:7a)

Believers do not become spiritually strong by eating religious garbage. They are commanded to "refuse" (*paraitou*)[6] constantly

4. The relative pronoun *hēi* ("whereunto") is feminine, singular, agreeing with its antecedent *didaskalias* ("doctrine").

5. Indicated by the perfect tense.

6. Present middle imperative, deponent.

that which would be detrimental to their souls. The verb stresses avoiding, declining, and rejecting (II Tim. 2:23; Titus 3:10).

Timothy had to refuse "fables" (*muthous*). The word transliterates as "myths" (cf. 1:4; II Tim. 4:4; Titus 1:14; II Peter 1:16). These are fallacious religious concepts that are illogically constructed from the Scriptures. They are described in two ways. First, they are "profane" (*bebēlous;* cf. 1:9; 6:20; II Tim. 2:16; Heb. 12:16). People profane sacred things when they go beyond that which the Scriptures teach or allow (Acts 24:6). They show their contempt for moral law by transgressing its limits willingly.

Second, these were "old wives' fables." This unique word (*graōdeis*) is a compound term composed of *graus* ("old woman") and *eidos* ("appearance").[7] The connotation is that of senility, futility, and weakness. These religious concepts drain spiritual energy, weaken the spirit, and are impotent to produce real vitality in the Christian life. They also imply legalistic traditions that are passed down from one generation to another.

2. Godliness involves exercise (4:7b)

The conjunction "and" (*de*) is a mild adversative designed to show the contrast between negative refusal and positive involvement. The imperative "exercise" stresses constant, strenuous activity that will increase strength and ability.[8] The English terms *gymnasium* and *gymnastics* are based upon the transliteration of the Greek word (*gumnaze*). The metaphor about calisthentics means that the believer must get into spiritual shape and then maintain that condition.

Personal responsibility is mandated by the reflexive pronoun ("thyself"). A believer cannot be a spectator in the spiritual experience; rather, he must become an active participant.

Olympic athletes trained to gain a corruptible wreath, but the goal of the Christian must be "unto godliness." Paul disciplined himself so that he could obtain the incorruptible crown of a victorious Christian life (I Cor. 9:24–27).

7. Used only here in the New Testament.
8. Present active imperative.

3. Godliness involves prcfit (4:8)

In an extension of the metaphor about exercise, Paul admitted that bodily exercise is profitable. This type of physical discipline has been viewed in three different ways. First, it denotes ordinary physical activity. Second, it may be a bodily exercise that proves to be a useful discipline for the soul and godliness. Third, it might be an ascetic discipline that has some personal benefit. The first view seems to be the most plausible.

Bodily exercise profits "little," literally "to little" (*pros oligon*). Kenneth S. Wuest says that it "extends to only a few things."[9] Homer A. Kent, Jr., suggests the translation "for a little extent and for a short duration."[10] There are some times in human life when physical strength is advantageous, but physical dexterity is not a prerequisite for success in all endeavors. As the mortal, corruptible body ages and weakens, the limitations of physical strength become very apparent.

In contrast, "godliness is profitable unto all things." A believer must apply biblical principles to all areas of behavior: in marriage, at work, and in all interpersonal relationships. Godliness has value in all that we do.

Godliness also has profit both in the present and in the future. Physical strength is limited to this life, but godliness is good for time and eternity. Christ came that believers might have abundant life (John 10:10). The best possible life that any person can live is in the will of God here and now. The blessedness of joy, peace, and satisfaction are part of the "promise of the life that now is."

At the judgment seat of Christ, the believer will be praised for his spiritual achievements, not for his physical accomplishments. Godliness is what counts in the life "which is to come."

II. THE MESSAGE OF A GOSPEL MINISTER (4:9-11)

This axiom was used earlier (1:15; 3:1). D. Edmond Hiebert believes that it went with the previous two verses (4:7-8),[11] although

9. *Word Studies in the Greek New Testament,* vol. 12, *The Pastoral Epistles* (Grand Rapids: Eerdmans, 1952), p. 71.

10. *The Pastoral Epistles* (Chicago: Moody, 1979), p. 157.

11. *First Timothy* (Chicago: Moody, 1957), p. 83.

it introduced two truths in the earlier references. The latter view seems to fit the context better. The axiom thus prepares the reader for the next verse (4:10).

A. The Atonement Must Be Proclaimed (4:10a)

The opening words ("for therefore") literally read "for unto this" (*eis touto gar*). They indicate the purpose for the ministries of both Paul and Timothy (note "we") and all other gospel preachers. The burden to preach redemptive truth affected two facets of their lives.

1. Labor

Preaching involved "labour" (*kopiōmen*). The emphasis here is on strenuous effort to the point of physical and emotional exhaustion. Paul put forth more effort than any other apostle (I Cor. 15:10). He labored night and day, preaching and making tents in order to support his missionary travels (I Thess. 2:9). He did this because he knew that his labor was "not in vain in the Lord" (I Cor. 15:58). His ministry was "in weariness and painfulness, in watchings often, in hunger and thirst, in fastings often, in cold and nakedness" (II Cor. 11:27). He desired to preach the gospel to those who had never heard because he knew that they could be saved only by faith in the proclaimed Word (Rom. 10:13–17; 15:20–21).

2. Reproach

This work produced "reproach" (*oneidizometha*).[12] The first verb points to what Paul did for others, whereas this second verb shows what some people did to him. He received verbal abuse, social ostracism, and physical beatings from the very people he tried to win to Christ. The focus of this term is upon verbal assaults and criticisms (Matt. 5:11; Mark 15:32). Christ was so reviled by the thieves who were on the crosses next to him, and all believers who manifest Christ in their lives will also be reviled (Mark 15:32; I Peter 4:14).

12. The critical Greek text has the verb *agōnizometha* ("we strive or agonize").

B. The Atonement Is Unlimited in Provision (4:10b)

The cause of Paul's and Timothy's evangelistic effort is indicated by the conjunction "because" (*hoti*). Two theological reasons are given.

1. God had saved them

The verb "we trust" (*ēlpikamen*)[13] means "we have placed our hope in God and we remain in that initial confidence." Elsewhere Paul wrote that "we are saved by hope" (Rom. 8:24). To hope in God and to believe in Him for salvation are synonymous.

The basis of the redemptive hope rests "in the living God." The preposition "in" (*epi*) normally is translated as "upon." God is the foundational rock *upon* whom the believing sinner places his hope for forgiveness of sins, the resurrection of the body, and deliverance from eternal punishment. Hope per se has no meritorious value. It is only as strong as the one upon whom it rests. Misplaced hope will bring disappointment and destruction. God is the "living" God, in contrast to the nonexistent gods upon whom the pagans at Ephesus had placed their confidence.

2. God can save others

The title "Saviour" (*sōtēr*) was a term of flattery given to authorities with political influence. It was given to princes who had benefited their countries. Later, it was ascribed to Caesar as the preserver of mankind and the protector of the Roman Empire. Many believers were martyred because they would not acknowledge Caesar to be their Savior and Lord.

The title "Saviour" is based upon the verb *save* (*sōzō*) and is applied equally to God the Father (1:1; Titus 3:4) and to Jesus Christ (Luke 2:11; Titus 1:4; 3:6).

In what sense can God be called "the Saviour of all men"? Four views have emerged. First, universalism teaches that God will eventually save all men. This position, however, repudiates the doctrine of eternal separation and punishment, which is clearly taught elsewhere.

13. Perfect active indicative.

Second, God is the preserver of all mankind in that He controls the seasons, the rain, the sun, and the air. The focus is on divine providence.[14] This view would be more plausible if God had been described as the Savior of "all things" (Col. 1:17) rather than "all men."

Third, the phrase has both a temporal and an eternal significance. For the unbelievers, it "includes preservation and deliverance from various evils and the bestowal of many blessings during this life."[15] For believers, it includes both present and eternal benefits (4:8).

Fourth, God is the Savior of all men in that He has provided redemption for all men in the crucifixion and resurrection of Jesus Christ.[16] He "sent the Son to be the Saviour of the world" (I John 4:14). Christ paid the price of redemption for all men, even those who denied Him (2:6; II Peter 2:1). He is "the propitiation . . . for the sins of the whole world" (I John 2:2). God reconciled the world to Himself through Christ (II Cor. 5:19). God loves the world (John 3:16) and wills all men to be saved (2:4). Only God can save and only He could provide the basis of salvation. If men want to be saved, they must trust only in Him.

C. The Atonement Is Limited in Application (4:10c)

There is a difference between provision of salvation and its appropriation. The limited phrase ("specially of those that believe") shows that the purpose of Christ's death was not to save all men but to provide redemption for those who believe in Christ. The value of Christ's death is extended to all, but it is realized only in believers.

D. The Atonement Must Be Communicated (4:11)

The two commands ("command and teach") grammatically could go with either the preceding verses or the following ones. Since the next section deals with personal imperatives directed by Paul to Timothy, it would be better to relate the two charges to the

14. Donald Guthrie, *The Pastoral Epistles,* Tyndale Bible Commentary (Grand Rapids: Eerdmans, 1972), p. 96.

15. Kent, *The Pastoral Epistles,* p. 159.

16. Author's view.

earlier truths that apply to the church (cf. 4:6, 8, 10). For example, why would Paul want Timothy to command and teach details about the latter's ordination (4:14)?

The first imperative, "command" (*paraggelle*), carries within it the ring of administrative authority, whereas the second charge, "teach" (*didaske*), stresses instruction in biblical doctrine. Both imply constant activity.[17]

III. THE EXAMPLE OF A GODLY MINISTER (4:12–16)

In this section, Paul put forth a series of eight commands. All stress constant compliance.[18] They point out qualities a minister should genuinely manifest to his people.

A. Integrity (4:12)

Two imperatives are set in contrast here by the use of the strong adversative "but" (*alla*). The first is negative and the second is positive.

1. Let no man despise your youth (4:12a)

Integrity is no respecter of age. A young person is as likely to have integrity as the senior citizen. The term "youth" (*neotētos*) could be used of anyone under the age of forty.[19] The writing of this epistle (A.D. 62–64) took place almost fifteen years after Timothy joined Paul's team during the apostle's second missionary journey (Acts 16:1–3; A.D. 49). The young associate, then, was at least thirty, probably closer to thirty-five.

The verb "despise" (*kataphroneitō*) literally means "to look down mentally" on someone. At stake was the dignity of Timothy's person and position. To carry out his assigned functions, he needed respect, not deprecation.

17. Both are present imperatives.

18. All eight are present imperatives.

19. Guthrie, *The Pastoral Epistles,* p. 97; Hiebert, *First Timothy,* p. 85; and Warren W. Wiersbe, *Be Faithful* (Wheaton, IL: Victor Books, 1981), p. 62.

2. Be an example (4:12b)

The command actually reads, "keep on becoming" (*ginou*). Timothy must not remain static as a role model, but should be constantly improving.

The term "example" (*tupos*) is the imprinted mark of a firm, heavy blow upon metal. Its verb form (*tuptō*) describes smiting or striking (Matt. 27:30; Luke 22:64). It is used of the nail prints in Christ's hands (John 20:25). Pastors should be examples to their people (I Peter 5:3). Paul was an example for others to follow (Phil. 3:17; II Thess. 3:9). So was Titus (Titus 2:7).

Six areas of exemplary life are listed.[20] First, Timothy was to become an example in his speech, both public and private ("word"). He must always speak the truth in love, marked by grace (Eph. 4:15; Col. 4:6).

Second, Timothy's lifestyle was to be praiseworthy. The connotation of the old English word "conversation" (*anastrophēi*) goes beyond speech to patterns of behavior (James 3:3; I Peter 3:1, 2, 16).

Third, the mention of "charity" or love (*agapēi*) deals with selfless giving through interpersonal relationships. Love for God must be seen in love for the people of God (I John 4:20–21).

Fourth, the phrase "in spirit" (*en pneumati*) probably refers to enthusiasm. A similar phrase, literally translated as "out of soul" (*ek psuchēs*) is given as the adverb "heartily" (Col. 3:23). The spirit is the self, the spiritual, mental, and emotional center of activity.

Fifth, Timothy must be trustworthy, a person in whom others should be able to place their faith and confidence. In addition, he must actively believe in God ("in faith"). The justified person must walk by faith, with childlike trust in the Word of God.

Sixth, Timothy must be an example "in purity" (*en hagneiai*). He must manifest a sinless, holy life of dedication before God and in his dealings with others (5:2). This concept was used of the Nazirite who consecrated himself to God (Num. 6:2, 21). The verb form is used of the purification of Jews before their religious feasts (John 11:55; Acts 21:24, 26; 24:18) and of the transformation of life from sin to holiness (James 4:8; I John 3:3).

20. Only five appear in the critical text. The phrase "in spirit" is omitted.

B. Commitment (4:13)

Paul earlier mentioned that he would return to Ephesus to rejoin Timothy (1:3; 3:14). The time of his coming was uncertain (3:15). During the period of the apostle's absence ("till I come"), Paul charged his associate to "give attendance" (*proseche*) to three areas of public ministry. This verb was used three times earlier (1:4; 3:8; 4:1). It indicates inner devotion and a total absorption in the task.

1. Reading

This command deals with the public reading of the Scriptures within the congregational services of the local churches.[21] Men must be told what God has said. Revival came to Israel after Ezra opened the book of the law and read it (Neh. 8:5, 8). Synagogue worship included the reading of the law and the prophets (Luke 4:16–20; Acts 13:15). Paul charged that his epistles be read in the churches (Col. 4:16). The entire Book of Revelation was to be read by all of the seven churches (Rev. 1:3–4). The Word of God must be central in ecclesiastical life. Neglect of it opens the door to moral and doctrinal apostasy.

2. Exhortation

The connotation of "exhortation" (*paraklēsei*) is sound exposition of the Scriptures which produces comfort, challenge, and change in the lives of the listeners. The noun is based upon a verb that means "to call beside." The Holy Spirit is the Paraclete, the one who consoles and encourages (John 14:16, 26; 16:7). Exhortation should result in decision.

3. Doctrine

The act of teaching is the essence of "doctrine" (*didaskaliai*). Teaching strengthens the intellect and the doctrinal understanding of the child of God. It gives proof. It differentiates between truth and error. When Ezra and his associates read the Old Testament Scriptures, they "gave the sense, and caused them to understand the

21. Kent, *The Pastoral Epistles,* p. 162.

reading" (Neh. 8:8). The result was joy among the people "because they had understood the words that were declared unto them" (Neh. 8:12).

The more devotion that a pastor gives to these three areas of pulpit ministry, the less chance that people will give heed to apostate error (4:1).

C. Use of the Gift (4:14)

The charge ("neglect not") implies that a Christian leader or believer can neglect to develop his potential. The verb literally means "be not careless about" (*amelei*). It denotes a lack of genuine concern. The verb was used of those who "made light of" the invitation to dinner (Matt. 22:5). A believer can show neglect of his salvation (Heb. 2:3). Neglect is described in three ways.

1. The ability was a gift

A gift ("the gift that is in thee") is an ability given to the Christian out of the grace of God through the Holy Spirit and controlled by the Spirit in Christian service and growth. The term "gift" (*charismatos*) is based upon the Greek term for "grace" (*charis*).[22] As a gift, ability is given apart from any merit within the recipient. The term is used for the gift of salvation (Rom. 5:15), the ability to function within the body of Christ (I Cor. 12:4, 9, 28, 30, 31), and a gift of money (II Cor. 1:11). It is never used as a synonym for the Holy Spirit.[23]

The prepositional phrase ("in thee") shows that the gift was not an appointed office such as that of pastor or apostolic delegate. This gift or ability was within Timothy; he was not within it.

The Holy Spirit is the divine agent by whom the gifts are distributed to every believer, although the triune God is involved in the operation (I Cor. 12:4–11). God alone decides what gift will be given to each one (I Cor. 12:11, 18). Christ, as the living head of the church, then gives the gifted men to the congregations for their edification (Eph. 4:11).

22. The term *charismatic* is based upon this word.
23. In Acts 2:38, the word *gift* is *dōrean.*

Believers are given their gifts either at the time of their salvation or at their conception. Timothy's enablement, however, was unusual. In the second epistle, Paul reminded his associate to "stir up the gift of God, which is in thee by the putting on of my hands" (II Tim. 1:6). As an apostle, Paul apparently had the authority to confer special gifts upon designated individuals who could assist him.

2. The gift was given through prophecy

The means of impartation was "by prophecy" (*dia prophēteias*). Wuest suggests that "prophetic intimations were given to Paul as to the selection of Timothy for the ministerial office."[24] The early church had prophets as well as apostles (Acts 11:27; 13:1; 21:10). The church was built upon the foundation laid by the two groups (Eph. 2:20; 4:11). Thus, one of these men who had both the gift of prophecy and the office of prophet could have pronounced a prophetic revelation about God's purpose for Timothy (cf. 1:18).

3. The gift was recognized

The giving of the gift was accompanied "with the laying on of the hands of the presbytery." The corporate noun "presbytery" (*presbuteriou*) includes the elders of the church at Lystra, Timothy's hometown, and possibly those at Iconium (Acts 16:1–2). The same word was used of the group of Jewish elders who opposed both Christ and the apostles (Luke 22:66; Acts 22:5).

There is no indication that the presbytery conferred the gift upon Timothy. That action was done by the Spirit through Paul (II Tim. 1:6). The presbyters' hands upon Timothy manifested their approval of him and recognition that God had equipped him for missionary service. They identified themselves with him in the work of the gospel.

D. Progress (4:15)

Two imperatives focus on goal orientation. The first deals with attitude and the second with action.

24. *The Pastoral Epistles,* p. 75.

1. The commands

First, the command "meditate" (*meleta*) is just the opposite of "neglect" (*amelei*). Timothy must have genuine concern about the things Paul had just enumerated.

Second, the imperative "give" literally reads "be in them" (*en toutois isthi*). Timothy's total interest and energy were to be invested in the ministry. The work of the gospel was to be his constant concern.

2. The purpose

The purpose for the two previous commands is indicated by the conjunction "that" (*hina*). The clause literally reads, "that your progress might be manifest in all things." The term *progress* (*prokopē*) literally means "to cut toward." It was a military term, used of engineers who would prepare a road for the advancing army by removing obstructions such as rocks and trees. Paul wanted Timothy to be a stronger role model for the church at the end of his Ephesian ministry than he was at the beginning. Such progress should be conspicuous in all areas of his behavior and performance.

E. Vigilance (4:16)

Believers must be sober and vigilant because Satan seeks to destroy them (I Peter 5:8). In this closing verse, Paul called Timothy to self-protection through two more commands.

1. The commands

The first command stresses attention. The imperative "take heed" (*epeche*) means "to hold upon, to fasten attention upon" (cf. Luke 14:7; Acts 3:5; Phil. 2:16). Two areas of personal oversight are listed: personal life ("thyself") and "doctrine." Timothy must be vigilant in his moral life and theology. Care for the man precedes care for the message, but both are equally vital. Personal sin usually leads to doctrinal error.

The second command emphasizes action. The believer, especially the pastor, needs staying power. Persistence and the determination to finish well are contained in the charge ("continue in them").

2. The result

The result of moral and doctrinal soundness for the preacher is a double salvation. First, he will save himself from personal and theological error by scriptural study and holy living. There is no hint that salvation from sin or hell is implied here. Salvation has multiple types in the Scriptures (2:15).

Second, the preacher will deliver his listeners from the same moral and doctrinal error if he lives and preaches correctly. Christians can become frustrated when they see their leaders fall into sin, and can be led into transgression through faulty teaching.

Questions for Discussion

1. What modern concepts compare with profane fables? How do these errors get started? How do they keep going?
2. In what areas is bodily exercise profitable? unprofitable? How much time and money should be invested in physical recreation?
3. How is godliness profitable in all areas? home? work?
4. Should unlimited or limited atonement become a doctrinal point for division of fellowship? How do the two views agree?
5. How can a young preacher demonstrate maturity to an older congregation? What disadvantages await a young minister?
6. What type of preaching should issue from the pulpit? evangelistic? expository? topical?
7. How do believers fall into moral and doctrinal error? What are the first signs of this weakness? How can these believers be rescued?

9

The Care of Widows

I Timothy 5:1-16

This section has two natural divisions: Timothy's relationships with various types of people within the church (5:1-2) and the responsibility of the local church to widows within its membership (5:3-16). Whereas the previous sections dealt with doctrine, this portion of the book is very practical.

I. INTERPERSONAL RELATIONSHIPS (5:1-2)

Pastors minister to people: men and women, boys and girls. They must treat each group properly. In this section, Paul identified four groups to whom Timothy would have to relate.

A. Men (5:1)

1. Older men

The term "elder" (*presbuterōi*) is used in a nontechnical sense of those who were older than Timothy. The apostle gave a similar charge to Titus: "But speak thou the things which become sound doctrine: That the aged men [same word] be sober, grave, temperate, sound in faith, in charity, in patience" (Titus 2:1-2).

Two guidelines are given to Timothy. The first is negative and the second is positive. The first is, "rebuke not" (*mȩ̄ epiplēxēis*) an elder.[1] The stress is on the prevention of such action.[2] The word

1. This verb is used only here in the New Testament.
2. Aorist subjunctive with negative.

literally means "upon a blow." Originally the term referred to fist-fighting, but it metaphorically meant "to censure severely," "to reprimand harshly," or "to beat down with verbal abuse." Younger men should never physically or verbally smite their elders.

Second, Timothy should "intreat him as a father." The verb "intreat" (*parakalei*) is the personal equivalent of the public exhortation (4:13). It involves a constant ministry of comfort and encouragement. Timothy must treat elders as a son honors his father (Eph. 6:2).

2. Younger men

Timothy must likewise entreat "the younger men as brethren." Paul told Titus, "Young men likewise exhort [same word] to be sober minded" (Titus 2:6). Although Timothy was an apostolic representative with delegated authority, he was still a brother in Christ and a member of the family of God. There is a difference between functional position and personal equality.

B. Women (5:2)

1. Older women

The phrase "elder women" (*presbuteras*) is the feminine equivalent of "elder" men. They must be treated as "mothers," with kindness, respect, and dignity.

2. Younger women

Two attitudes toward younger women are mentioned. First, Timothy was to deal with younger women "as sisters." Second, his personal contact with them must be "with all purity" (same word as 4:12).[3] Here is a specific application of the general principle. There must be no suspicion of sexual impropriety in Timothy's associations with women who are possible candidates to be his wife.

3. D. Edmond Hiebert applies the prepositional phrase to all four groups. See *First Timothy* (Chicago: Moody, 1957), p. 90.

II. THE SUPPORT OF WIDOWS (5:3–16)

Widows have a prominent part in the New Testament. Christ criticized the Pharisees for taking advantage of helpless widows (Matt. 23:14), commended the widow for her sacrificial gift of two mites (Mark 12:41–44), showed compassion on the mourning widow and resurrected her dead son at Nain (Luke 7:11–18), and utilized the importunity of the wronged widow as an illustration of persistent prayer (Luke 18:1–8). Anna, a widow for eighty-four years, saw the infant Christ and prophesied concerning Him (Luke 2:36–38).

The word "widow" (*chēra*) denotes one who is bereft, robbed, and has suffered loss. The connotation is that of loneliness and emptiness.

A. Distinction Between Types of Widows (5:3–8)

A widow is a woman whose husband has died. However, there are different types of widows: those with no family whatsoever (5:3), those who have family (5:4, 8), godly widows (5:5), sinful widows (5:6), older ones (5:9), and younger ones (5:11).

1. *Widows with no family (5:3, 5–6)*

The imperative "honour" (*tima*) includes both parental respect and financial support. If only respect were meant, then why should only one group receive it? The essence of honor is to appreciate the value of someone. Christ criticized the Pharisees because they dishonored their parents by their failure to render monetary assistance to them (Matt. 15:3–6).

The general principle is to honor "widows that are widows indeed." The adverb "indeed" (*ontōs*) could be translated as "truly" or "genuinely." It is reinforced later by the addition of the verbal adjective "desolate" (*memonōmenē*). This term literally means "one who has been permanently left alone."[4] She is the only one in her family still alive.

The specific principle is to honor genuine widows who are also

4. Perfect passive participle. Note the word *mono* in it.

godly believers (5:5). She must have two marks of spirituality. First, she has placed her hope upon God (*ēlpiken epi ton theon;* cf. 4:10). She must be a genuine Christian, one whose confidence for spiritual and physical preservation rests in God. She looks to Him to meet all of her needs. Second, she must be concerned about others. She cannot be characterized by self-pity and selfish anxiety. Rather, she must "continue in supplications and prayers night and day." The revered Anna was such a woman. She "departed not from the temple, but served God with fastings and prayers night and day" (Luke 2:37). This action does not imply twenty-four hours of prayer every day. She begins and ends her day with prayer for others. She faithfully attends the meetings of the congregation.

A genuine widow, however, can disquality herself from ecclesiastical honor (5:6). A widow who "liveth in pleasure" (*spatalōsa*) is one who uses her available money in riotous and luxurious living. In her remorse, bitterness, and loneliness, she may have tried to drown her sorrows in sinful pleasures. She gave up hope and saw no further reason for living. In that sense, she "is dead while she liveth." She has physical and spiritual life, but she has forfeited the enjoyment of the abundant life (John 10:10) by her self-centeredness. James criticized the wealthy for the same wasteful lifestyles: "Ye have lived in pleasure on the earth, and been wanton" (James 5:5; same word).[5] The church cannot subsidize a widow who misuses her money in this way. The church must exhort her to repent. If she fails to respond, then she becomes ineligible. This disciplinary action is necessary in order to bring her back to the practices of godly living and widowhood.

Timothy had an administrative responsibility to make the distinction known to the entire church (5:7). The purpose for such admonition is indicated by the conjunction (*hina;* "that"). The goal is that "they may be blameless." The plural verb may refer only to the sinful widows (5:6), to the children who must provide support (5:4), or to the entire church family. The last seems most plausible in that all people must know what is expected of them and all widows must understand what they can expect from their families and the church. The adjective "blameless" (*anepilēptoi*), used earlier

5. This verb occurs only in these two verses.

of the pastor (3:2), shows that no believer should be delinquent in his financial concern for family members who have need. James wrote, "Pure religion and undefiled before God and the Father is this, To visit the fatherless and widows in their affliction, and to keep himself unspotted from the world" (James 1:27). The essence of Christianity is loving and giving. John offered this penetrating observation: "But whoso hath this world's good, and seeth his brother have need, and shutteth up his bowels of compassion from him, how dwelleth the love of God in him?" (I John 3:17). A blameless attitude toward widows is seen in loving words supported by deeds of financial assistance (I John 3:18).

2. Widows with family (5:4, 8)

The second group of widows has living family members. Two types of relatives are listed. The first are the "children" (*tekna*), the sons and daughters of the woman. The second are her grandchildren. The term translated as "nephews" (*ekgona*) is better rendered as "grandchildren."[6] They are "the begotten out of her ones." The term is based upon a verb that means "to come to be out of" (*ekginomai*). Nothing is said about the widow's sisters, brothers, uncles, aunts, or cousins, unless the family term (*ekgona*) includes them also. If so, then the term would indicate anyone related to the widow who could trace his family tree back to someone who was the common ancestor of both of them.

The family members have three responsibilities to the widow. First, they must "learn first to shew piety at home." Genuine discipleship involves family responsibilities. Reverence for God must be seen through respect for parents (*eusebein;* "piety"). This term, in its noun form, is used eight times in this epistle as "godliness" (2:2; 3:16; 4:7, 8; 6:3, 5, 6, 11). The same verb is applied to the Athenians who worshiped (same word) the unknown god (Acts 17:23). Believers must meet the financial needs of their own family members before they contribute to a benevolent fund in their church.

Second, these family members must "requite their parents." The verb means "to render recompense," "to reward," or "to pay back"

6. Used only here in the New Testament.

(*amoibas apodidonai;* cf. Matt. 6:4; 18:28). They must give from themselves to the widows. Solomon wrote that "a good man leaveth an inheritance to his children's children" (Prov. 13:22). It is logical to conclude that children would support their needy parents after those parents had invested their time, energy, and money in their children (II Cor. 12:14). The term "parents" (*progonois*) identifies the progenitors, those who are physically responsible for the existence of the children. Care for parents manifests a beautiful family relationship and is "acceptable before God" (5:4b).

Third, each believer must provide "for his own, and specially for those of his own house" (4:8a). The first phrase includes all relatives and possibly the church family, whereas the second deals with the immediate family. The verb "provide" (*pronoei*) stresses the concept of thought beforehand. The believer must perceive the needs of the family and plan in advance to meet those needs.

Two criticisms are leveled against the believer who refuses to make ample provision for his family (4:8b). First, he "has denied the faith" in that he does that which is contrary to the essence of Christianity. God saw the need of the sinful human race and He gave His Son to meet that need. The denial does not imply the loss of spiritual justification. Second, such a believer "is worse than an infidel." This term literally means an "unbeliever" (*apistou*). Many cultures and religious groups, although unsaved, nevertheless revere their elders and provide for their needs until death.

B. Qualifications of Enrolled Widows (5:9–10)

What was the nature of the enrollment specified by the command, "Let not a widow be taken into the number"? The verb (*katalegesthō*) means "to set down on a list or a register," thus "to enroll."[7] This church action definitely revealed planned provision (cf. 5:8).

Three views about the enrollment of these widows have been put forth. The first is that the roll is a list of the genuinely destitute widows who received financial aid from the church. This view suits the context, but it also introduces some problems. Would not the church help a desolate widow who was under sixty years old? The qualifications for support had already been given (5:3, 5).

7. Used only here in the New Testament.

The second interpretation is that these widows are deaconesses. If this were the case, then why did Paul not use the word *deaconess* rather than "widow"? Could only widows qualify as deaconesses? Why should they begin their work at age sixty?

Third, the most plausible view is that these widows constituted a special order of Christian workers in the church. In the historical development of the postapostolic church, an order of female presbyters emerged. Their duties were to care for the orphans and to give counsel to the younger women. They were ordained and took the vow of perpetual widowhood. This order was eventually dissolved by ecclesiastical action at the Council of Laodicea (fourth century). These widows thus rendered spiritual work for the financial assistance they received.

Various qualifications had to be met before the widows could be enrolled.

1. Age (5:9b)

The widow had to be at least sixty years old.

2. Marital history (5:9c)

The widow must be "the wife of one man." Literally, the phrase reads "a one-man woman" (*henos andros gunē*). This is similar to the requirement for the pastor (3:2).

Three interpretations of this phrase have developed. First, there could be no second marriage after the death of the husband if the widow expected to be put on this list eventually.[8] However, if this prohibition against a second marriage existed, why did Paul order a second marriage for younger widows? These younger widows would automatically be disqualified when they took their second husbands. This situation creates an incongruity.

Second, the widow lived "chastely in the marriage relation."[9] She was never guilty of adultery.

8. Donald Guthrie, *The Pastoral Epistles,* Tyndale Bible Commentary (Grand Rapids: Eerdmans, 1972), p. 102; A. T. Robertson, *Word Pictures in the New Testament,* (Nashville: Broadman, 1931), vol. 4, p. 585; and Kenneth S. Wuest, *Word Studies in the Greek New Testament,* vol. 12, *The Pastoral Epistles* (Grand Rapids: Eerdmans, 1952), p. 82.

9. Hiebert, *First Timothy,* p. 95.

Third, the widow was never divorced.[10] Just as the pastor could not have a history of divorce, neither could an enrolled widow.

3. Service (5:10)

The widow's sphere of activity must be in "good works" (*en ergois kalois*). Although such righteous deeds are basically a private matter between the believer and God (Matt. 6:1-18), at the same time they become visible to others. Secret spirituality will manifest itself in public performance. A widow thus must be "well reported" (*marturoumenē*) by others. Solomon wrote, "Let another man praise thee, and not thine own mouth" (Prov. 27:2). Dorcas exemplified this type of woman. She was "full of good works and almsdeeds which she did" (Acts 9:36). After she died, the widows of her city showed Peter "the coats and garments which Dorcas made, while she was with them" (Acts 9:39).

Five areas of good works are cited. They are all introduced by the conditional particle "if" (*ei*).[11] First, the widow had to be a good mother ("if she have brought up children"). Apparently her children had all died by this time. If she cared for orphans, then they also were dead.

Second, the widow was hospitable ("if she have lodged strangers"). Jesus commended those who offered hospitality (Matt. 25: 35-44). The apostles claimed that believers should be "given to hospitality" (Rom. 12:13) and that they should offer it "without grudging" (I Peter 4:9). Many gracious people opened up their homes: Simon the tanner (Acts 10:6), Lydia (Acts 16:15), Philip (Acts 21:8), Mnason (Acts 21:16), Publius (Acts 28:7), and Gaius (Rom. 16:23).

Third, the widow was courteous and humble ("if she have washed the saints' feet"). Both the sinful woman and Mary washed the Savior's feet (Luke 7:36-40; John 12:3). They demonstrated their love and gratitude through this action. This act of kindness was a private matter, not a constant participation in an ordinance.[12]

10. Warren W. Wiersbe, *Be Faithful* (Chicago: Moody, 1981), p. 70. This is the author's view.

11. Some scholars have suggested these five areas represent five questions that were asked of the widow at the time of her enrollment interview.

12. Homer A. Kent, Jr., who is Grace Brethren, sees this as an ordinance participation. See *The Pastoral Epistles* (Chicago: Moody, 1979), pp. 173-174.

Fourth, the widow was compassionate ("if she have relieved the afflicted"). She gave sufficient aid to those who were in physical and emotional distress. She was concerned with the needs of others even though she had needs of her own. She was one who bore the burdens of others (Gal. 6:2; Phil. 2:4).

Fifth, the widow actively pursued the godly life ("if she have diligently followed every good work"). Her strength and interest were all aimed in the right moral direction.

C. Rejection of Younger Widows (5:11–15)

The group of "younger widows" refers to those who were probably under forty years of age (cf. 4:2; 5:2).[13] The adjective "younger" (*neōteras*) is based upon the word *new* (*neos*). It could be that the younger widows were those whose husbands recently died (compare the reference to new [i.e., freshly made] wine in Luke 5:37).

As the general supervisor of the work at Ephesus, Timothy was to "refuse" (*paraitou;* see also 4:7) the admittance of these younger widows into the group of widows who worked for the church.

1. The problem (5:11–13)

Two reasons are given for refusing the younger widows' requests. First, they still had the desire to marry (5:11–12). Paul anticipated a time when these women's sexual and emotional impulses toward another marriage would return ("for when they have begun to wax wanton against Christ"). The verb "wax wanton" (*katastrēniasōsi*) is used elsewhere of Babylon the great and the earthly kings who "lived deliciously" together (Rev. 18:7, 9). Elsewhere Paul gave this counsel to widows: "It is good for them if they abide even as I. But if they cannot contain, let them marry: for it is better to marry than to burn" (I Cor. 7:8–9). There was no guarantee that these younger widows could "contain" this inner compulsion for male companionship.[14] Their attraction to men superseded their commitment to serve Christ and the local church permanently.

13. Note that the three words used for youth are based upon the same stem (*neos*).
14. The term "when" (*hotan*) should be read as "whenever."

The main verb ("they will marry") should be translated as "they constantly will to marry" (*gamein thelousin*). These younger widows had the persistent desire for marriage even though they may not have married a second time. This unrevealed desire actually brought a judgment (*krima*)[15] upon them in that they wanted financial support from the church while they were still seeking mates. The cause for this criticism was that "they have cast off their first faith."[16] The verb (*ēthetēsan*) means "to reject," "to set aside," or "to nullify." The phrase ("the first faith") does not refer to redemptive faith that secures eternal salvation; rather it points to their initial pledge of remaining unmarried after being widowed. If marriage followed this commitment, then their word would prove to be untrustworthy.

The second reason for refusal was possible idleness (5:13). Since these widows were younger and stronger than the older widows, they could work to support themselves. When they were given financial support, however, they soon discovered that they had too much free time. In that sense, they "learn to be idle." The inference is not that they were idle when they were married, but that they could learn to be so if the church supported them financially. The adjective "idle" (*argai*) literally means "no work" (cf. Matt. 20:3, 6).[17]

Four aspects of possible idleness are given. First, these widows were "wandering about from house to house." Widows, employed and supported by the church, apparently went from house church to house church and from one widow's house to another in the performance of their service. This activity, however, could be misused if a woman simply visited for her own social pleasure. Visiting the widows and gadding about are not synonymous (cf. James 1:27). Second, these women could become "tattlers" (*phluaroi*).[18] The verb form was used of Diotrephes, who was "prating against [John] with malicious words" (III John 10). The metaphor is that of water boiling up, of bubbles being formed. In her access into many private lives, the widowed worker could easily become a gossip, fomenting trouble as she spread empty charges. Third, these women could

15. The translation "judgment" is preferable to "damnation."
16. Note the causal conjunction "because" (*hoti*).
17. The adjective is made up of *ergon* ("work") and the *alpha* prefix.
18. Used only here in the New Testament.

become "busybodies." This term literally means "around work" (*periergoi*). She circumvented genuine spiritual work with her feminine social interests. The latter could easily have included conversation about possible candidates for a husband and ways to contact these men. Fourth, the widows could be "speaking things which they ought not." These were things that were not necessary in the execution of the widows' ministry (*ta mē deonta*). The heretical legalists plagued the churches with this same harmful speech (Titus 1:11).

2. The need (5:14–15)

Paul could not force widows to marry against their wishes; however, he could issue apostolic directives that provided the wisest counsel for the widows to follow. His will ("I will," *boulomai;* cf. 2:8) provided the best solution to the predicament (note "therefore"). His opinion was logical and spiritual.

Paul desired four goals for the widows who still felt the need for male companionship.[19] First, he wanted them "to marry" (*gamein*). In his analysis of the social situation, he knew that their gift of marriage had to be satisfied (Matt. 19:10–12; I Cor. 7:8–9).

Second, Paul desired these widows "to bear children" (*teknogonein*). It may be that the younger widow produced no children in the first marriage, perhaps due to the sterility of her husband. The presence of children would give her deliverance from personal uselessness (cf. 2:15). She could fill her time with the spiritual admonition of her children (Eph. 6:4). In her later years, she could receive financial support from these children who then would be adults.

Third, Paul wanted the widows "to guide the house" (*oikodespotein*). She literally is the "house despot or lord." The virtuous woman "looketh well to the ways of her household, and eateth not the bread of idleness" (Prov. 31:27). She is in charge of food, clothing, and shelter (Prov. 31:10–31). She uses household means to assist the needy (Prov. 31:20).

Fourth, Paul wanted these widows to quell all possible criticism by the unsaved ("to give none occasion to the adversary to speak reproachfully"). The term "occasion" (*aphormēn*) is a military

19. All four verbs are infinitives.

metaphor, referring to a base of operations. Paul did not want the unsaved adversary to criticize the cause of Christ because of the carnal, hypocritical behavior of unfulfilled widows.

Unfortunately, some younger widows had "already turned aside after Satan." This probably refers to either the violation of the standards (5:11–13) or immoral conduct. The latter could even include marriage with unsaved men. The reference to "Satan" means an attitude or action with which Satan is in total agreement. Christ thus said to Peter, "Get thee behind me, Satan: thou art an offence unto me: for thou savourest not the things that be of God, but those that be of men" (Matt. 16:23). When men and women choose the selfish instincts of natural men over divine priorities, they turn aside after Satan.

D. Support of Widows (5:16)

This verse may serve as a conclusion to the discussion of younger widows (5:11–15) or to the treatment of the entire subject (5:1–15).

1. The condition

Every human being should care for his widowed mother, widowed grandmother, or any widowed relative who has no means of support. This responsibility is heightened for Christians. The conditional clause ("if any man or woman that believeth have widows") assumes the reality of this situation.[20] This obligation rests equally upon a believing man or woman.[21] It is possible that one believer might have to provide for two or more widows in his family.

2. The commands

Two imperatives are given. First, let the believer "relieve" the widows (cf. 5:10). He must render complete financial assistance to her. Second, "let not the church be charged." This verb (*bareisthō*) stresses that which is weighty, heavy, and burdensome. Paul worked as a tentmaker so that he would not be a financial burden to the churches (I Thess. 2:6).

20. Note the usage of *ei* ("if") with the indicative verb (*echei*).
21. The critical Greek text omits the reference to the believing man (*pistos*).

3. The result

When a believer takes care of the widows in his family, that releases the church to "relieve them that are widows indeed." These widows, of course, are those who have no living family members and are too old to remarry or to find employment.

Questions for Discussion

1. How should modern families care for their widows? Is a nursing home biblically acceptable?
2. How do pensions and Social Security fit into the financial support of widows today? What standard of living should be acceptable to a widow?
3. Should a widow continue to live in her home after the death of her husband? Should she move into a retirement home? into the home of one of her children?
4. How can widows effectively serve God today? What unique ministries can they have?
5. How can your local church better serve the needs of its widows? What needs to be done? How can a church reach out to unsaved widows in the community?
6. Should churches hire widows to perform certain tasks? What should they be paid?
7. Should a church discipline a member who gives no assistance to a needy widow? How could this problem be solved?

10

The Problem of Elders

I Timothy 5:17-25

Instructions about the financial support of the widows served as a fitting transition to comments about the monetary expectations of the elders. Paul had earlier discussed the qualifications of the elders (3:1-7); now he wanted to inform the church, through Timothy, about the elders' salaries, discipline, and ordination.

I. SUPPORT OF THE ELDERS (5:17-18)

The "elders" (*presbuteroi*) are those who hold the office of bishop-pastor-elder (3:1), not the ones who are aged (5:1).

A. Basis of Support (5:17)

The church was instructed to financially support the elders for their spiritual ministry within the church. Two spheres of work are mentioned.

1. The elders' rule

The elders must "rule well" (*kalōs proestōtes*). The verb literally means "to stand before." An elder is an administrative officer who stands before the congregation to preside over its activity. The gift of ruling is an ability endowed by the Holy Spirit for use within the body of Christ (Rom. 12:8). An elder is "over" (same word) the church "in the Lord" (I Thess. 5:12). This is a functional, ecclesiastical authority, not a personal supremacy or superiority. This verb also stresses the fact that the elder has ruled so well in the past that the good effects of his work can still be seen in the present life of the church.[1] This use of the perfect tense rather than the present (found in Rom. 12:8; I Thess. 5:12) suggests that these men may have been senior elders who no longer were actively involved in administrative duties.

The adverb ("well") discriminates between mediocrity and excellence. It implies promptness and orderliness (Rom. 12:8).

2. The elders' labor

The adverb "especially" (*malista;* cf. 4:11) indicates that "they who labour in the word and doctrine" are also among those who rule. Homer A. Kent, Jr., observes that "this verse does not give sufficient warrant for the Reformed view of two classes of elders, those who ruled and those who taught."[2] If these elders were, in fact, rather old, then the verse means that they were still preaching and teaching even though they gave up administrative duties. The principle, of course, would apply equally to any elder who was actively engaged in the total pastoral work.

The connotation of "labour" (*hoi kopiōntes*) is hard work and wearisome toil. Labor involves a maximum expenditure of time and energy. It is full time, not part time.[3] The place of labor is within the congregation, not outside of it (cf. I Thess. 5:12; "among you").

The sphere of labor is marked by both preaching and teaching ("in the word and doctrine"). No article appears before "word" (*en logōi kai didaskaliai*); therefore, the noun refers to an oral proclamation of the gospel rather than to the written Word of God. The elders naturally studied the Scriptures in order to declare them. The first term ("word") relates to their ministry to the unsaved, whereas the second focuses on the instruction of believers. The elders' sphere of concern was similar to that of the apostles, who confessed that they would give themselves continually "to prayer and to the ministry of the word" (Acts 6:4).

1. The verb is a perfect active participle.
2. *The Pastoral Epistles* (Chicago: Moody, 1979), p. 181. D. Edmond Hiebert, *First Timothy* (Chicago: Moody, 1957), p. 101, agrees.
3. The verb is a present active participle.

B. Type of Support (5:17a)

The command is that the elders "be counted worthy of double honour." A worthy person who performs a worthy task should be esteemed as worthy by others. That worth should be both qualitative and quantitative. He should receive "double honour" (*diplēs timēs*), but what does that mean? Various views have been put forth.

First, the elder should receive a double portion of food at the love feast that preceded the ordinance of the Lord's Table. Second, he should receive twice as much money as the "widow indeed." Third, the phrase simply means he receives an ample or generous salary.[4] Fourth, the elder should gain double respect: once for his age and once again for his pastoral office. Fifth, he should receive one honor for his position and another for service with distinction.[5] Sixth, he should obtain respect, both implicit and explicit, from the church, plus a living wage.[6] Elsewhere Paul charged, "And we beseech you, brethren, to know them which labour among you, and are over you in the Lord, and admonish you; And to esteem them very highly in love for their work's sake" (I Thess. 5:12-13).

C. Reason for Support (5:18)

The explanatory conjunction "for" (*gar*) gives the main reason for double honor. The basis of all faith and practice must be "the scripture" (*hē graphē*). In the theological conviction of the biblical authors, "God says" and "the Scripture says" were synonymous (Acts 1:16; 28:25). Paul constantly referred to the canonical Word as the absolute proof of a doctrinal assertion (Rom. 4:3; 9:7; 10:11; 11:2; Gal. 4:30). The use of the singular shows that Paul united an Old Testament verse from the Mosaic law with a recorded quotation of Christ within the Gospel of Luke under the single title of "scripture." Both utterances were equally authoritative. All sixty-six books, written by forty different men, are actually one book given by God. The Bible is His Word.

4. Donald Guthrie, *The Pastoral Epistles*, Tyndale Bible Commentary (Grand Rapids: Eerdmans, 1972), p. 105.
5. Hiebert, *First Timothy*, p. 101.
6. Author's view.

1. Old Testament Scripture

The first quotation came from the Mosaic law (Deut. 25:4). At first, it seems strange that Paul used a verse that dealt with the humane treatment of oxen that were used in work. Elsewhere, he used this same quotation in his argument that preachers should be given financial support (I Cor. 9:8–9). He then gave this rhetorical and logical inference: "Doth God take care for oxen? Or saith he it altogether for our sakes? For our sakes, no doubt, this is written" (I Cor. 9:9–10). He proceeded to point out that temple priests were supported by the people, then concluded, "Even so hath the Lord ordained that they which preach the gospel should live of the gospel" (I Cor. 9:14). Pastors should receive material support, whether money, food, clothing, shelter, or all of them, for their spiritual ministries (I Cor. 9:11).

2. New Testament Scripture

The second quotation is from Jesus Christ, contained within the Gospel of Luke (Luke 10:7). When Christ sent out the seventy preachers, two by two, He informed them that they would be dependent upon the financial generosity of their listeners for their subsistence (Luke 10:4–6). He added, "And in the same house remain, eating and drinking such things as they give: for the labourer is worthy of his hire. Go not from house to house. And into whatsoever city ye enter, and they receive you, eat such things as are set before you" (Luke 10:7–8). He gave the twelve apostles the same counsel when He sent them out on their first preaching mission (Matt. 10:9–13).

The adjective "worthy" (*axios*) in the quotation is based upon the verb earlier mentioned (*axiousthōsan;* "be counted worthy").

II. REPUTATION OF THE ELDERS (5:19–21)

Elders are human. As such, they are not above sin, wrongdoing, or criticism. Even the early church at Jerusalem was marked by murmuring members who complained that some administrative functions were performed with partiality (Acts 6:1). Paul thus wanted Timothy and the church to know how to handle a situation when an elder would be accused of sin.

A. Protection Against a False Charge (5:19)

Discipline played a prominent part in the life of the early church. Ananias and Sapphira were stricken with instantaneous, premature death by God through the apostolic authority of Peter when they hypocritically lied to God and the church (Acts 5:1–11). Christ outlined the threefold procedure of reconciliation before excommunication could be effected: personal confrontation, testimony of witnesses, and action of the entire church (Matt. 18:15–19). Other discipline included avoidance (Rom. 16:17–18), deliverance to Satan (I Cor. 5:5), expulsion and removal of fellowship (I Cor. 5:11–13), withdrawal (II Thess. 3:6, 14), separation (II Tim. 2:21–26), and rejection (Titus 3:10). The goals of such action are the spiritual health of the church (I Cor. 5:7), restoration (Gal. 6:1–3), and forgiveness (II Cor. 2:6–11). Discipline is like surgery. It hurts at the time, but the patient will be better for it.

As members of a church, elders are not immune to the procedure of discipline. The same standards apply to them as well as to the laymen.

1. The command (5:19a)

Paul stated, "Against an elder receive not an accusation." The imperative "receive" (*paradechou*) means "to welcome with total acceptance" (Mark 4:20; Acts 16:21; 22:18; Heb. 12:6). Members could make their complaints directly to Timothy as the general overseer of the work. If one member kept bringing the same charge against one elder without any substantiation, Paul wanted Timothy to stop that. The command literally reads, "Stop receiving as you have been doing."[7] No further hearing was to be given to such unilateral attacks.

One qualification for an elder is that he be "not accused of riot or unruly" (Titus 1:6). The "accusation" (*katēgorian*) mentioned in this verse probably refers to that specific type of sin. It seems to be a

7. The prohibition uses *mē* with the present imperative.

formal accusation presented to the church, other elders, and Timothy. Others had such legal charges leveled against them: Christ by the Jewish leaders before Pilate (Luke 23:14); Paul by the Jewish multitude (Acts 22:30); Paul by Tertullus before Felix (Acts 24:2); and believers by Satan before God (Rev. 12:10). Paul, by personal experience, knew what it meant to be falsely accused; thus he chose this term wisely.

2. *The exception (5:19b)*

The accusation could be received if it rested upon the testimony of "two or three witnesses." The preposition "before" (*epi*) should be translated as "upon." An accusation against an elder must have the corroboration of two or three who would agree.

This principle is based upon the directive in the Mosaic law: "At the mouth of two witnesses, or three witnesses, shall he that is worthy of death be put to death; but at the mouth of one witness he shall not be put to death" (Deut. 17:6). Moses later added, "One witness shall not rise up against a man for any iniquity, or for any sin" (Deut. 19:15). In fact, the punishment for that sin fell upon the false witness (Deut. 19:16–21). Christ confirmed this procedure, saying "that in the mouth of two or three witnesses every word may be established" (Matt. 18:16). Paul also used this concept in his admonition to his critics at Corinth (II Cor. 12:14; 13:1).

B. Rebuke for a True Charge (5:20)

1. *Objects of the rebuke*

The phrase "them that sin" (*tous hamartanontas*) refers to the elders,[8] although it is possible that it could refer to church members who brought false accusations against the elders. The verb form stresses habitual sin in the performance of the office.[9] The focus is on sin that is a violation of divine moral law, not upon some inefficiency or incompetence in performing pastoral tasks.

8. Kent, *The Pastoral Epistles,* p. 185.
9. It is a present active participle.

2. Nature of the rebuke

The imperative "rebuke" (*elegche*) means more than a reprimand; it denotes an admission of guilt and the subsequent conviction of the sinner. The errant elder must become aware of his wrong and be convinced of it. This same verb is used of the Holy Spirit who "reprove[s] the world of sin, and of righteousness, and of judgment" (John 16:8). The Bible itself is profitable for "reproof" (II Tim. 3:16; same word). In the second epistle, Paul charged his associate to "reprove" the listeners when he preached the Word (II Tim. 4:2). Titus was given similar directions (Titus 1:9, 13; 2:15). In the key passage about discipline, the same verb is used in the italicized portion: "Moreover if thy brother shall trespass against thee, go and *tell* him his *fault* between thee and him alone" (Matt. 18:15; italics added).

3. Circumstances of the rebuke

The rebuke was to be given "before all." Public sin requires public rebuke, especially when leadership is involved. The phrase could possibly be limited to apply to all elders,[10] but it is better to interpret it as a reference to the entire church, with both elders and members present.

4. Purpose of the rebuke

The rebuke was to arrest the sin of the elder, to produce repentance within him, and to restore him to a productive ministry. Beyond that personal benefit was a corporate lesson to learn. The rebuke was necessary "that others also may fear." The term "others" (*hoi loipoi*) refers primarily to the other elders who witnessed the rebuke. They needed to know that the practice of sin within their awesome position of spiritual administration could not be tolerated. The pastorate provides neither a pretext nor an excuse for sin. In another sense, the entire church needed to realize the importance of a leadership without reproach. After God disciplined Ananias and Sapphira with instantaneous physical death, "great fear came upon all the church, and upon as many as heard these things" (Acts 5:11).

10. Hiebert, *First Timothy*, p. 103.

C. Guarantee of Fair Treatment (5:21)

It is difficult to determine whether this verse goes with the preceding two verses or with the following. The principle contained within it could easily apply to both discipline and ordination.

1. The charge of Paul

The opening appeal ("I charge") speaks of solemn testimony (Acts 20:24; 23:11; I Thess. 4:6). Paul gave a similar charge in the second epistle (II Tim. 4:1). The verb is used of Peter (Acts 2:40), Peter and John (Acts 8:25), Paul (Acts 18:5), the Holy Spirit (Acts 20:23), and of Timothy himself (II Tim. 2:14).

The purpose of the charge was "that thou observe these things," the things just discussed (5:19–20). It would be difficult for Timothy to rebuke publicly a church elder, especially since that officer would be older than the associate. Paul told Timothy earlier not to rebuke a senior citizen (5:1), but he could rebuke a person in an official position. This latter rebuke is functional and administrative, not personal. The verb "observe" (*phulaxēis*) means "to guard" or "to protect." Paul had to encourage his timid friend to obey this difficult directive.

2. The presence of God and angels

Paul wanted Timothy to know that the latter was under observation. The elders and the church were watching (5:20); these were human. Now the apostle informed his associate that he was being viewed by the supernatural world as well. First, the appeal was given "before God."[11] The preposition literally means "in the sight of" (*enōpion*). The Father sees the proceedings (II Tim. 4:1).

Second, the "Lord Jesus Christ" was also a divine witness. As the living head of the church, He wanted His authority to be manifested (I Cor. 5:4). As the chief shepherd, He has a perfect right to command His undershepherds (John 21:15–17; I Peter 5:1–4).

Third, the mention of the "elect angels" is noteworthy. These are

11. The Granville Sharp rule may apply here. If so, the terms "God" and "Lord" refer to the same divine person. However, both may be seen as proper names (II Tim. 4:1).

the angels who have completely obeyed God since their creation. They were chosen by God unto Himself when He allowed Satan and evil angels to sin and to fall from their original estate of probationary holiness. Angels are curious about God's redemptive program for the human race (I Peter 1:12). God is teaching the angels about His wisdom through His dealings with the church (Eph. 3:10). Just as angelic leaders were disciplined for their sins of insubordination, so human leaders should also be chastised for their sins.

3. The absence of prejudice

Timothy had to obey the charge with two proper dispositions. First, he had to follow instructions "without preferring one before another." The phrase literally reads "apart from prejudgment" (*chōris prokrimatos*).[12] Timothy should not make a judgment about the accusation before all of the facts were set forth. He had to suspend a verdict of guilt or innocence until he had a thorough understanding of the situation.

Second, Timothy should do "nothing by partiality." This term (*prosklisin*) denotes an inclination toward someone.[13] Within the family of God and the performance of the ministry, it is easy to have fondness toward some and little tolerance for others. Timothy, however, could not give preferential treatment to his friends. He could not give them the benefit of the doubt if the weight of evidence was against them.

III. ORDINATION OF THE ELDERS (5:22-25)

The apostles laid hands on the first seven deacons who were chosen by the Jerusalem church to care for the widows (Acts 6:5-6). During the first missionary journey, Paul and Barnabas "ordained them elders in every church" (Acts 14:23). The apostle instructed Titus to "ordain elders in every city, as I had appointed thee" (Titus

12. Used only here in the New Testament.
13. Used only here in the New Testament.

1:5). Timothy himself had hands laid upon him by both the presbytery and Paul (4:14; II Tim. 1:6).

Invested with authority by Christ, the apostles directly ordained elders from those who qualified and who desired the position. The apostles then delegated this authority to their official representatives. This action was necessary in the formative years of the church. Since the apostles and their associates have passed from the scene, the responsibility for the ordination of elders has passed to the local churches, which must follow the inscripturated guidelines.

A. The Commands (5:22a)

Two commands are given. The first is objective; the second is subjective.

1. Avoid quick decisions

The first command prohibits impromptu action: "Lay hands suddenly on no man." The adverb (*tacheōs*) denotes quickness.[14] Much prayer, thought, counsel, and examination must precede appointment. Christ prayed all night on the mountain before He chose the twelve apostles (Luke 6:12–13). Quick decisions are usually wrong. They are based primarily upon peer pressure or superficial observation. Samuel made this faulty judgment when he initially assumed Eliab was God's choice for king (I Sam. 16:6–7).

The laying on of hands signifies the ordination of new elders,[15] although some scholars identify the laying on of hands with the restoration of repentant elders[16] or the reconciliation of sinning members.[17]

2. Avoid participation in sin

The second command warns against wrong recommendations: ". . . neither be partaker of other men's sins." Ordination implies

14. The word *tachometer,* referring to an instrument that measures revolutions per minute (RPM), is based upon this adverb.

15. Kent, *The Pastoral Epistles,* p. 187.

16. A. T. Robertson, *Word Pictures in the New Testament* (Nashville: Broadman, 1931), vol. 4, p. 589.

17. Kenneth S. Wuest, *Word Studies in the Greek New Testament,* vol. 12, *The Pastoral Epistles* (Grand Rapids: Eerdmans, 1952), p. 87.

approval of the candidate's doctrinal convictions, moral character, and ability to execute the position of pastor. Any subsequent failure on the part of the new pastor could fall back upon those who initially recommended him.

John cautioned the elect lady against permitting apostate teachers to preach within her house church. He gave this counsel: "If there come any unto you, and bring not this doctrine, receive him not into your house, neither bid him God speed: For he that biddeth him God speed is partaker of his evil deeds" (II John 10–11).

B. The Example (5:22b–23)

1. In general reputation (5:22b)

Paul earlier charged Timothy to be an example "in purity" (4:12). Now, he again admonished, "Keep thyself pure." This purity could extend to the proper discipline and ordination of elders (5:19–22). It could also emphasize a characteristic of the ideal Christian leader in all situations.

2. In personal need (5:23)

Timothy apparently was in poor health from time to time. In Ephesus, years before, God had "wrought special miracles by the hands of Paul" (Acts 19:11). When Paul's work aprons were placed upon the infirm, their diseases departed. There was no special miracle available for Timothy, however. The need for miracles declined as the authenticated ministry of the apostles was established.

Paul thus gave some medical counsel in two commands. First, "drink no longer water." In that culture, water was often unsanitary. To avoid the charge of addiction to wine (3:3), Timothy chose to abstain totally from wine. He drank only water. This command therefore did not call for total abstinence from water, but for a relaxation from drinking water only.

Second, Paul advised Timothy to "use a little wine." He did not command Timothy to become a wine drinker. Timothy was to use wine medicinally by mixing it with water to produce a non-intoxicating, sanitary drink.[18]

The preposition "for" (*dia*) introduces two reasons for the medicinal use of wine. First, Timothy had a weak stomach ("for thy stomach's sake"). Someone has suggested that he should use wine for a weak stomach, but not to make his stomach weak. Second, he had "often infirmities." The presence of sickness is not an indication of sinfulness in life. In many cases, disease is the natural result of living in a mortal, corruptible body. The infirmities were not a part of divine chastisement, because Paul later identified Timothy as a man of God (6:11). He had many "infirmities" (note the plural) and he had them "often."

C. The Evaluation (5:24–25)

Guthrie believes that these two verses logically follow verse 22, and that verse 23 is parenthetical.[19] Regardless, the emphasis on the contrast between sins and good works shows that much care should be exercised in the ordination process.

1. Sins (5:24)

The principle elucidated in this verse is true of all believers, but its primary application is to pastors. Three assertions are made about sins. First, the sins of some men are "open beforehand" (*prodēloi*). The word literally means "to show" or "to manifest in advance." These sins are public, obvious, and conspicuous. The term is translated elsewhere as "evident" (Heb. 7:14).

Second, the sins are "going before to judgment." This "judgment" (*krisin*) probably refers to the trial of a sinning pastor and his subsequent loss of position. It is a judgment in this life.

Third, some sins "follow after" men. They constitute a part of their guilty consciences until the time of their deaths. These sins may or may not be discovered by men after the person's decease.

18. For more information on the mixing of wine and water in ancient times, consult Norman L. Geisler, "A Christian Perspective on Wine-Drinking," *Bibliotheca Sacra,* vol. 139, no. 553, pp. 46–56. See also Robert H. Stein, "Wine-Drinking in New Testament Times, *Christianity Today,* June 20, 1975, pp. 9–11.

19. *The Pastoral Epistles,* p. 108.

Regardless, the pastor will have to face the consequences of those secret sins at the judgment seat of Christ (II Cor. 5:10).

2. *Good works (5:25)*

The connective "likewise" (*hōsautōs*) shows that the same is true of good works. Two statements are given about them. First, the good works of some "are manifest beforehand" (*prodēla*). The ministries of some spiritual pastors are recognized even during their lifetimes. Such men receive their double honor: the respect, love, and confidence of their people plus the financial support they richly deserve.

Second, the productive ministries of some pastors go unnoticed and often unappreciated by their people. In these instances, the omniscient God will reward them openly at the judgment seat. These good works "cannot be hid."

Questions for Discussion

1. How can the ministries of pastors or elders be evaluated properly? What criteria should be used?
2. In what ways can a congregation honor its pastor? Why do some pastors feel unappreciated?
3. How much salary should be given to a pastor? How often should he get a raise? What about cost-of-living increases? pensions? health insurance?
4. What are the priorities of a biblical, pastoral ministry? How can laymen assist the pastor to accomplish these goals?
5. How do churches show partiality toward their leaders? How can prejudice be avoided?
6. How can ordination be revoked? What sins disqualify a pastor from continuing in his position?
7. How do pastors hide their sins? Why do some good ministries go unnoticed?

11

The Error of False Doctrine

I Timothy 6:1–10

The closing chapter of the epistle contains teaching about several topics: the attitudes of Christian slaves toward their owners (6:1–2), the peril of false teachers (6:3–10), the directives about Timothy's own life and ministry (6:11–16), the admonition to wealthy Christians (6:17–18), and the warning against Gnostic speculation (6:19–21). The book ends as it began, with an apostolic charge (6:13, 17; cf. 1:3).

I. THE DUTIES OF SLAVES (6:1–2)

Although the Bible nowhere directly attacks the institution of slavery, principles for the humane treatment of slaves are found in several epistles (Eph. 6:5–9; Col. 3:22—4:1; I Peter 2:18–25). Slaves were to be treated as people, not as property. Paul usually gave counsel to both the slave and the slave owner, but in this passage the commands are directed toward the slaves only. Two major relationships of the Christian slave are examined: the first with unsaved owners and the second with believing masters.

A. Duty to Unsaved Masters (6:1)

The term "servants" (*douloi*) does not refer to free men who hired themselves out as domestic workers. Rather, in that first-century culture, these people were slaves, owned as chattel property. They thus could be bought, sold, or exchanged. The additional phrase ("as are under the yoke") indicates a difficult situation. They were treated like oxen. In the Roman world of the first century, the slaves were mostly Gentiles. Rarely was a Jew a slave or a slave owner. These slaves heard the gospel and became believers. Although they had spiritual freedom in Christ, they still were in social bondage with legal responsibilities to their owners (I Cor. 7:20–24).

1. The command

The command to slaves was to "count their own masters worthy of all honour." This command has two features. First, the recipients of respect were "their own masters." This term (*despotas*) transliterates as "despot." It denotes "absolute ownership and uncontrolled power."[1] It is ascribed to both God the Father and the Lord Jesus Christ (Acts 4:24; II Peter 2:1; Jude 4; Rev. 6:10).

Second, the nature of respect was "worthy of all honour." Both widows and elders were to be honored by believers (5:3, 17). The honor given to the owner was based upon the position he held, not his harsh character. The concept of worth comes from a recognition of authoritative headship within a culture or society. In the same sense, believers should "honour the king" even if that ruler is immoral, as the pagan Caesar was (I Peter 2:17).

2. The reason for the command

The reason is introduced by the purpose conjunction "that" (*hina*). Quality work and humble obedience by Christian slaves would prevent a legitimate occasion for blasphemy by their unsaved masters and pagan observers. The Gentiles blasphemed the God of Israel because of the nation's unbelief, idolatry, and disobedience (Rom. 2:24).

Two objects of blasphemy were to be avoided. First, Paul did not want "the name of God" to be blasphemed. The name of God stands for all that He is. The very essence of the triune divine Being could suffer reproach through the insubordination of believing slaves.

Second, the apostle did not want the "doctrine" (*hē didaskalia*)

1. Kenneth S. Wuest, *Word Studies in the Greek New Testament*, vol. 12, *The Pastoral Epistles* (Grand Rapids: Eerdmans, 1952), p. 90.

to be blasphemed. If the first concept points to the person of God, then this term refers to the program of God as expounded in the Scriptures. What God is and how He acts can become targets of ridicule if Christians do not manifest proper interpersonal relationships. The reception of salvation in Christ should make any person, whether slave or free, a more responsible citizen and worker.

B. Duties to Saved Masters (6:2)

Slave owners, when they became Christians, did not instinctively set their slaves free. Christian slave owners did not immediately set slaves free when the latter themselves became believers. The relationship between spiritual brothers, one an owner and another a slave, thus became sensitive and confusing. What actions and attitudes should each manifest toward the other? Paul here gave two directives to the saved slave.

1. Do not despise your master (6:2a)

The prohibition (*mē kataphroneitōsan*) literally means "not to think down." Although the slave was spiritually equal to his saved master, the former could be tempted to pour mental contempt upon his owner for the latter's failure to release the slave from social bondage. In that sense, he saw himself as spiritually superior to his master. The slave probably reasoned that, since both he and the owner were delivered from bondage to sin, the owner should follow Christ's example and free the slave. The same verb is used of children being despised by the disciples (Matt. 18:10), the riches of divine goodness by the unsaved (Rom. 2:4), the church by divisive Christians (I Cor. 11:22), Timothy's youth by the church (4:12), the shame of the cross by Christ (Heb. 12:2), and government by the apostates (II Peter 2:10).

The reason for maintaining a proper attitude is "because they [the masters] are brethren." Brothers should not despise each other. The social error of the owner could not be overcome by the bitterness of the slave. It is never right to do wrong to another. Paul wanted Philemon to treat the runaway slave, Onesimus, like a "brother beloved" (Philem. 16). The slave should look upon his saved owner as a beloved brother also.

2. Serve your master (6:2b)

The connective words ("but rather") show the strong contrast between the two imperatives. The negative sinful attitude must be replaced by positive, holy action. The command stresses constant, daily service that a slave is expected to perform (*douleuetōsan*).[2]

The reason behind the directive is somewhat ambiguous. The phrase literally reads, ". . . because faithful and beloved are the ones who lay hold of the good work." Are these the slaves or the masters? The parallelism with the first part of the verse would indicate this applies to the slave owners. The "benefit" (*euergesias*) does not refer to spiritual redemption.[3] Wuest believes that masters will take hold of good service in beneficial activity toward slaves who obey.[4] A more plausible explanation is that Christian masters who receive good work from their saved slaves are faithful and beloved in the opinion of the slaves. Christian slaves must serve, not "with eye-service, as menpleasers; but in singleness of heart, fearing God" (Col. 3:22). They must view themselves "as the servants of Christ, doing the will of God from the heart; With good will doing service, as to the Lord, and not to men" (Eph. 6:6-7).

Paul then charged Timothy to "teach" these concepts to the church members, especially the believing slaves.[5]

II. THE PRIDE OF A FALSE TEACHER (6:3-10)

The book ends as it began, by dealing with the threat of heretical doctrine. In the first chapter, legalism was mentioned and refuted, but there is silence in the last chapter. If the same error is under discussion, the context of the false teaching was stressed earlier, but in this section the character of the false teachers is set forth. It is

2. Present active imperative.

3. Homer A. Kent, Jr., *The Pastoral Epistles* (Chicago: Moody, 1979), p. 191.

4. *The Pastoral Epistles,* p. 91.

5. The critical Greek text places the two commands ("teach and exhort") at the beginning of the new paragraph (6:3-10).

possible that these teachers were pastors who wrongly used their office for financial gain.

A. The Conditions of Pride (6:3)

The conditional particle "if" (*ei*) does not introduce a hypothetical situation; rather, it presents a real-life predicament within the church.[6] The use of the indefinite, singular pronoun (*tis;* "any man") conveys the sweeping apostolic indictment against any present or future heretic. Two basic faults are presented.

1. The heretic teaches error

Constant teaching of error, not an isolated instance of doctrinal defection, is stressed here.[7] To "teach otherwise" (*heterodidaskalei*) is to advocate heterodoxy (cf. 1:3).[8] Such teaching involves the proclamation of another gospel that is devoid of redemptive truth (Gal. 1:6–9). It denies salvation by grace through faith alone. It may accept the historical facts of Christ's death and resurrection, but it sets up a sacramental means by which the value of that redemptive work is mediated to the recipient.

2. The heretic rejects truth

The false teacher does not "consent" to redemptive truth. The verb literally means "to come to" (*proserchetai*). He is aware of the truth, but he refuses to approach it. He will not attach himself to it.

The adjective "wholesome" (*hugiainousi*) was earlier translated as "sound" (1:10; cf. Titus 1:9, 13; 2:1, 2). The English term *hygiene* is based upon it. The adjective stresses that which is healthy and complete. Paul later warned Timothy about church members who would not endure "sound doctrine" (II Tim. 4:3). This concept is further clarified by two absolute standards. First, sound doctrine represents "the words of our Lord Jesus Christ." This could refer to

6. The usage of *ei* with the two indicative verbs shows that Paul was describing reality.
7. The verb is present active indicative.
8. The only two uses of this verb in the New Testament are in this book (1:3; 6:3).

either what Christ Himself spoke or oral and written teaching about Him.[9] Both naturally complement each other. Such truth is life-giving and life-edifying (John 6:63; II Tim. 3:15–17). Second, sound words manifest "the doctrine which is according to godliness." This must issue in holy, righteous living. Truth, properly taught and believed, radically transforms both the teacher and the disciple. Believers must both know and do the truth.

B. The Characteristics of Pride (6:4–5)

The attitudes and actions of the false teacher are now set forth in a descriptive series.[10] The main verb ("he is proud") conveys the metaphorical impression that the false teacher has completely inflated or puffed himself up (*tetuphōtai*).[11] He is like a balloon that is fully blown up. Paul earlier condemned the sudden promotion of a new believer into a position of leadership because pride could overcome the latter (3:6). One of the marks of the apostates in the last days is that they will be "highminded" (II Tim. 3:4; same word). God hates the "proud look" (Prov. 6:17). A person puffed up with self-importance is on the brink of spiritual self-destruction.

1. Conceited ignorance

A proud religionist really is marked by "knowing nothing." The verb (*epistamenos*) means that he is "unable to do any concentrated or reflective thinking."[12] The word *epistemology* (denoting a division of philosophy) is based upon this term. An Arabian proverb states, "He who knows not and knows not that he knows not: he is a fool, shun him." Such men are "ever learning, and never able to come to the knowledge of the truth" (II Tim. 3:7).

2. Spiritual sickness

The participle "doting" (*nosōn*) conveys the idea of being sick.[13] Its noun form (*nosos*) is always translated as "sickness" (Matt. 4:23),

9. The former interpretation views the word "Christ" as a subjective genitive, whereas the latter sees the term as an objective genitive.
10. The various descriptions actually relate to the only main verb ("he is proud").
11. Perfect passive indicative.
12. Wuest, *The Pastoral Epistles*, p. 92.
13. The verb is used only here in the New Testament.

"disease" (Luke 4:40), or "infirmities" (Luke 7:21). Since the false teacher rejected a diet of "wholesome words" (6:3), he logically succumbs to the attack of two sinful viruses. The first is "questions" (*zētēseis*). Constant mental inquiry, prompted by an autonomous ego, is spiritually counterproductive. Such questions are foolish and never issue in godly edification (1:4; II Tim. 2:23; Titus 3:9). The second involves "strifes of words" (*logomachias*). The false teacher literally generates "word wars." Paul later commanded Timothy to preach, "charging them before the Lord that they strive not about words to no profit, but to the subverting of the hearers" (II Tim. 2:14). Spiritual semantics destroy genuine vitality and purpose.

3. Personal conflicts

The connective "whereof" (*ex hōn*) literally means "out of which things." This phrase refers to the questions and conflicts over words. Sinful attitudes come out of mental disputes caused by pride. A proud teacher looks upon all others as threats to his positional security.

Five types of wrong responses are given. The first is "envy" (*phthonos*). A proud person is jealous about the success of others and the attention that is drawn away from himself. Envy is a work of the flesh (Gal. 5:16, 21, 26; I Peter 2:1). It is an expression of the unsaved life, although Christians also are capable of envying (Rom. 1:29; Phil. 1:15).

The second response is "strife" (*eris*). A proud person puts down others and contradicts them in order to elevate himself. Strife is the result of envy. Envy is the emotion; strife is the expression of that emotion. It also is a work of the flesh (Gal. 5:20) and a manifestation of the unsaved life (Rom. 1:29; "debate"). It was the main sin that caused the divisions within the church at Corinth (I Cor. 1:11; "contentions").

The third reaction is "railings" (*blasphēmiai*). The word transliterates as "blasphemies." A proud teacher verbally assaults those who disagree with him and those who do not submit to his leadership.

The fourth response is "evil surmisings." This noun (*huponoiai*) literally means "underthoughts." It points to malicious suspicions. A proud teacher is insecure, suspicious of all who could threaten his leadership. He conjures up evil suppositions within his imagination.

The fifth response is "perverse disputings" (*paradiatribai*).[14] The English word *diatribe* is based upon this term. The imagery is of thorough, mutual irritation or friction caused by constant rubbing. In personal conflicts, this attitude issues in bitter and violent verbal attacks upon an adversary. Such attacks are full of angry criticism and denunciation.

4. *Perverted minds*

The disputings arise from men marked by two sinful qualities. First, these people are "men of corrupt minds." Donald Guthrie states that "when reason is morally blinded, all correctives to unworthy behavior are banished, and the mind becomes destitute."[15] Their corrupted mental state was permanent.[16] Only a divine work of spiritual resurrection could deliver them.

Second, these sinful men are also "destitute of the truth." The verbal adjective "destitute" (*apesterēmenōn*)[17] indicates that such a person has been defrauded or robbed of the truth. He is spiritually bankrupt. Truth has been taken away from him; only error remains.

5. *Materialistic*

The false teacher wrongly supposes that godliness is gain.[18] He believes that intellectual religiosity and reverent respect are means to gain financial support. His biblical knowledge is for hire.

Paul then charged Timothy to "withdraw" (*aphistaso*) from such false teachers.[19] Separation from error is necessary to maintain moral and doctrinal purity (Rom. 7:17–18; II Cor. 6:11—7:1).

14. The critical Greek text spells this word *diaparatribai.*

15. *The Pastoral Epistles,* Tyndale Bible Commentary (Grand Rapids: Eerdmans, 1972), p. 112.

16. The word "corrupt" is a perfect passive participle (*diephtharmenōn*).

17. Perfect passive participle.

18. This is the proper translation. The subject of the verb is "godliness" and the predicate nominative is "gain."

19. This phrase is not found in the critical Greek text ("from such withdraw thyself").

C. The Cause of Pride (6:6–10)

Solomon cautioned his people, "A man's pride shall bring him low" (Prov. 29:23). In spite of this wise counsel, egotistical men have structured their own destruction through selfish pursuits.

1. Ignorance of the nature of contentment (6:6–8)

Paul set forth three principles of life that the greedy teachers either rejected or ignored. First, success is spiritual and inward, not material and outward (6:6). The apostle took the erroneous statement of the false teachers, corrected it, and applied it to his readers. Christ promised the abundant life (John 10:10). Thus a believer not only can have "gain" (*porismos*) in this life, but also "great" gain. Gain is achieved through "godliness with contentment." The noun "contentment" (*autarkeias*) is a compound word based upon "self" (*autos*) and "to be sufficient" (*arkeō*). It denotes an inward satisfaction that is not affected by outward circumstances. It is rooted in faith in divine sufficiency (II Cor. 9:8). Greedy teachers minister to receive, but a spiritual leader wants to give. Believers must learn "to be content" in whatever financial situation they find themselves (Phil. 4:11). Neither the abundance nor the shortage of money should affect their spiritual growth.

Second, an understanding of the exact nature of life recognizes the superiority of the eternal and spiritual to the temporal and material (6:7). Material things, such as food, clothing, shelter, and money, are necessary for survival and for the enjoyment of earthly life. A person, however, "brought nothing into this world," and "can carry nothing out."[20] Life begins and ends with the absence of material possessions. Spiritual purposes therefore should not be centered in or measured by objective, material accumulations. Jesus Christ warned, "Take heed, and beware of covetousness: for a man's life consisteth not in the abundance of the things which he possesseth" (Luke 12:15). Job maintained his spiritual integrity when he lost everything. He properly exclaimed, "Naked came I out of my mother's womb, and naked shall I return" (Job 1:21). He blessed the name of God because he knew that God can sovereignly take away

20. The word "nothing" is emphasized, since it appears first in the sentence.

from man what He has graciously given to him. Both David and Solomon made this same observation (Ps. 49:17; Eccl. 5:15).

Third, possession of the basic necessities of life should foster contentment (6:8). The term "food" (*diatrophas*) is actually plural.[21] It is based upon a verb that means "to support" or "to nourish thoroughly" (*diatrephō;* cf. Matt. 6:26; Acts 12:20). The term thus encompasses all foodstuffs necessary to support life. The noun "raiment" (*skepasmata*) is also plural and can encompass both shelter and clothing.[22] It literally means "coverings." The verse seems to end with an exhortation ("let us be content"), but the verb really indicates an assertion of realized contentment (*arkesthēsometha*).[23] It should be translated, ". . . we shall be content." Paul and his associates had already learned that God alone could meet their needs (II Cor. 12:9).

2. Desire to be rich (6:9)

Three observations can be made. First, the people are "they that will be rich" (*hoi boulomenoi ploutein*). It is not immoral to be wealthy. Many godly men were also rich (e.g., Abraham, David, and Solomon). It is wrong, however, when the desire to become rich is so persistent and overwhelming. The phrase literally translates as "the ones who are daily wishing to become rich." This sin can be committed by anyone, regardless of his degree of financial success.

Second, the plight of such aspirants is that they "fall" (*empiptousin*). The same verb was used of the pastor who can fall if he is not mature and spiritual (3:6–7). The imagery is that of an animal falling into a pit from which it cannot extricate itself (Matt. 12:11; Luke 14:5). This verb, however, conveys the idea of repeated falls.[24] This person fails to learn his lesson. Each new scheme to get rich issues in a new fall. These people literally fall "in" (*en* prefix on verb) and "into" (*eis*) three different types of spiritual pits. The first is "temptation" (*peirasmon*). When a wrong motivation and an occasion to gain money come together, the natural response is sinful submission to that temptation. It is not sinful to be tempted per se,

21. Used only here in the New Testament.
22. Used only here in the New Testament.
23. It is future passive indicative, not the hortatory subjunctive.
24. Present active indicative.

because Christ was tempted. However, giving in to the temptation to sin must always be blamed on self and Satan. The second pit is a "snare" (*pagida;* cf. 3:7). It is a trap set by the devil. The third pit is "many foolish and hurtful lusts." These "lusts" (*epithumias*) are intense passions that control the emotional and psychological drives of the individual. They are "foolish" (*anoētous*) in that they occur without proper thought behind them. They are also foolish in that they "do not yield the promised satisfaction."[25] The lusts are also "hurtful" (*blaberas*) in that they are harmful to self, family, and all others touched by the frenzied pursuit of wealth. Such fanaticism for temporal, material pleasures destroys the very characteristics that reflect the image of God within man.

Third, the false teachers' punishment is twofold. Their lusts will "drown" (*buthizousi*) them. This same verb is used of the boats that began to sink in the Sea of Galilee because of the weight of the extra fish (Luke 5:7). The irony behind the desire to be rich is that the riches men want in order to go to the top are the very burdens that bring them to the bottom. These people are unwittingly on a downward course toward spiritual ruin. The first punishment is "destruction" (*olethron*) in this life. It involves dissipation, emotional and mental disorders, bankruptcy, and family loss. The second judgment is "perdition" (*apōleian*), a reference to the future life. It refers to eternal torment in the lake of fire (Matt. 7:13; Rom. 9:22). If the term is applied only to this life, then it points out the terrible waste of time and effort (Matt. 26:8).

3. Love of money (6:10)

Money per se is not evil; it is morally neutral. It can be either a curse or a blessing, depending on the motivation behind its use. What is immoral is "the love of money" (*hē philarguria;* cf. 3:3). The phrase literally reads "the love of silver." When a person loves money for its own intrinsic value, then it becomes wrong. It no longer is a good means to a good end; rather, it has become an evil end in itself.

Three ill effects of the love of money are given. First, it is "a root

25. D. Edmond Hiebert, *First Timothy* (Chicago: Moody, 1957), p. 114.

of all types of bad things" (*rhiza pantōn tōn kakōn*).[26] It is not *the* root of *all* evil. From it, however, does spring up a variety of problems. Because of it, men steal, defraud, exploit, and lie.

Second, men have "erred from the faith" as they have reached out for wealth. They literally have been led astray away from (*apeplanēthēsan*) the body of redemptive truth ("the faith"; cf. 3:9). They have been deceived by satanic riches. The latter phrase refers to the exposition of the person and redemptive work of Jesus Christ, not to personal belief. The verb "coveted after" (*oregomenoi*) was earlier translated as the "desire" for a pastoral office (3:1). In his eager straining for wealth, this person becomes difficult to reach with the gospel message. He wants the riches of this world, not the riches of divine grace. Of him Christ could say, "For what is a man profited, if he shall gain the whole world, and lose his own soul?" (Matt. 16:26). He is like the myopic rich fool (Luke 12:16–34).

Third, such people have self-inflicted spiritual, mental, and emotional wounds. They have "pierced themselves through with many sorrows." The sorrows include a guilty conscience, sad memories, and broken friendships. The quest for money can never produce the abundant life that Christ promised. Joy comes only when a life is centered in God and in others, not in cold metals.

Questions for Discussion

1. What principles, based upon the directives to the slaves, can be applied to the relationship between employers and employees? What are the main differences between slaves and employees? similarities?
2. How do cults and sects reject orthodox doctrine? How do they disguise their error?
3. What contemporary theological disputes are fruitless? Why do evangelicals permit them to go on?
4. In what ways has religion been used for financial gain? Can religious racketeers be stopped? How?

26. Literal translation.

5. Are Christians too materialistic? What is a simple lifestyle? How much money is enough?

6. What specific sins occur when the desire to be rich takes over? How have some people been destroyed through this desire?

7. What is the love of money? How can it be detected? avoided?

12

The Final Charge

I Timothy 6:11–16

The contrast between Timothy and the greedy false teachers had to be as conspicuous as the difference between white and black. In these closing verses of the epistle, Paul gave his associate a series of four commands (6:11–12) followed by an awesome charge (6:13–16).

I. THE MARKS OF SPIRITUALITY (6:11–12)

The paragraph begins with a double address. First, the opening words ("But thou"; *su de*) were used to capture Timothy's attention. The personal pronoun (*su*) is definitely used for emphasis.[1]

The second phrase is unique: "O man of God" (*Ō anthrōpe tou theou*).[2] The exclamatory particle (*Ō*) is used with only two proper names: Timothy and Theophilus (Acts 1:11). The title ("man of God") was used in the Old Testament for Moses (Deut. 33:1), Samuel (I Sam. 9:6), Elijah (I Kings 17:18), and David (Neh. 12:24). The Scriptures have the ability to turn a saved child into a man of God (II Tim. 3:17). The Scriptures were written by "holy men of God" (II Peter 1:21). Although Timothy was seen as a youth by the church (4:12), Paul called him a man of God. He was a person whose life was centered in God and controlled by Him. Timothy, who was likeminded to Paul, could also confess that the essence of life is Christ (Phil. 1:21; 2:20). In contrast with the greedy teachers, who

1. Used only here in the epistle.
2. Used only here in the New Testament.

were men of gold, Timothy was a man of God. Scriptural motivations dominated his life.

A. Flee (6:11a)

Constant, deliberate flight from all forms of sin and immorality should mark the life of a believer. The command to flee (*pheuge*)[3] denotes daily obedience. It could be translated as "keep on fleeing" or "flee habitually." The phrase "these things" (*tauta*) is emphasized here.[4] It refers to the sins of the false teachers and the destructive temptations that were just discussed (6:3–10).

Elsewhere, Paul charged believers to flee fornication (I Cor. 6:18), idolatry (I Cor. 10:14), and youthful lusts (II Tim. 2:22). A child of God must separate himself from the moral pollution of the world, but he cannot isolate himself from the immoral people of the world. He must seek to win the lost fornicator without yielding to the temptation of fornication. To accomplish this task, he must heed the admonition: "But put ye on the Lord Jesus Christ, and make not provision for the flesh, to fulfil the lusts thereof" (Rom. 13:14).

The imagery conveyed by the command to flee is that sinful practices are chasing the believer constantly. To avoid being caught, the believer must develop and maintain moral stamina. Joseph fled the enticements of Potiphar's wife (Gen. 39:12), but David fell into the immoral trap of his own making (II Sam. 11:1–4). The imperative indicates personal accountability for successful obedience or sinful disobedience.

B. Follow (6:11b)

The first command dealt with negative behavior, but this second imperative aims at producing positive spirituality. A believer not only must run *from* sin, but also must run *to* moral goodness. Unfortunately, some Christians flee without following, whereas others follow without fleeing. To flee and to follow are both necessary.

3. Present active imperative.

4. The phrase grammatically appears before the imperative; thus, "these things flee."

The command "follow after" (*diōke*) is often translated as "persecute" (Matt. 5:10; John 15:20; Gal. 1:13). This latter concept stresses aggressive pursuit in order to apprehend the object. The idea behind the command to follow, then, involves determination, persistence, total energy, and purposefulness. This pursuit must be a daily drive.[5] Elsewhere, the Scriptures charge the children of God to follow hospitality (Rom. 12:13; "given" is the same word), peace and brotherly edification (Rom. 14:19), love (I Cor. 14:1), the purpose of divine calling (Phil. 3:12, 14), the good (I Thess. 5:15), peace and holiness (Heb. 12:14; I Peter 3:11).

Six objects of pursuit are given.

1. Righteousness

There are three types of righteousness. The first is an essential attribute of God. Only He is righteous in and of Himself. The second is positional righteousness, which the believing sinner has in Christ (Phil. 3:9). In Christ, therefore, he can be declared righteous or justified. The third is practical righteousness. John wrote, "If ye know that he is righteous, ye know that every one that doeth righteousness is born of him" (I John 2:29). Paul appealed for Timothy to develop this third type. Each believer has the daily responsibility to develop a righteous character before God and man.

2. Godliness

This is the eighth and final use of this term in this epistle (2:2; 3:16; 4:7, 8; 6:3, 5, 6, 11). The word denotes general piety and holy conduct. It stresses devotion to God through worship and reverence.

3. Faith

Sinners are justified by faith in Jesus Christ (Rom. 5:1; Eph. 2:8-9). There is a difference, however, between saving faith and sustaining faith. The latter involves the daily walk of the child of God. This type of faith is gained through a knowledge of the written Word of God and an unquestioning obedience to it (Rom.

5. The verb is a present active imperative.

10:17; Heb. 11:6). Faith is the opposite of sight (II Cor. 5:7). This faith trusts God for success when sight only sees defeat.

4. Love

The love of money is a natural expression of the sinful urges within man, but the believer needs to follow genuine "love" (*agapēn;* cf. I Cor. 14:1). At conversion, believers "are taught of God to love one another" (I Thess. 4:9), but they must work at increasing and abounding that love (I Thess. 4:10; II Thess. 1:3). One fruit of the Spirit is love (Gal. 5:22). The objects of this love must always be God, fellow believers, and members of one's natural family, but never the immoral principles and practices of the pagan world (I John 2:15–17).

5. Patience

The term "patience" (*hupomonēn*) is a compound word meaning "to remain under" (*menō* and *hupo*). A person is patient when he remains steadfast under the difficult pressures of life. It is a biblical axiom that "tribulation worketh patience" (Rom. 5:3). It is "not therefore so much a passive acceptance of the inevitable, as an active unrelenting endeavor even in spite of difficulty and trial."[6]

In this verse, patience may also refer to the confident expectation of the return of Christ in one's own lifetime (II Thess. 3:5). His coming is mentioned later in the passage (6:14).

6. Meekness

The essence of "meekness" (*praiotēta*) is not weakness; rather, it is power under control.[7] An ox within a yoke is meek, able to be turned in any direction by the will of its master. Meekness is the opposite of insubordination. Moses, Christ, and Paul were all meek (Num. 12:3; Matt. 11:29; I Cor. 4:21). This virtue is marked by courtesy and a spirit of quiet submission (Gal. 6:1; Col. 3:12). It is a fruit of the Spirit (Gal. 5:23).

6. Herbert M. Carson, *The Epistles of Paul to the Colossians and to Philemon,* Tyndale Bible Commentary (Grand Rapids: Eerdmans, 1960), p. 37.

7. The critical text uses another term (*praupathian*) translated as "meekness."

C. Fight (6:12a)

The command to "fight" (*agōnizou*) focuses on both the defense and the propagation of the biblical doctrine of redemption. The imperative, based upon the imagery of an athletic contest or a military conflict, is transliterated as "agonize." The verb connotes strategy, strength, and stamina. Paul used the verb elsewhere for the effort expended to gain spiritual mastery in the disciplined life (I Cor. 9:25), for his "striving" to present every believer perfect in Christ (Col. 1:29), and for the fervent labor of Epaphras in his intercessary prayers (Col. 4:12). At the close of his apostolic ministry, Paul could confidently assert, "I have fought a good fight" (II Tim. 4:7). He had evangelized the lost, discipled believers, established churches, and defended the truth against the attacks of apostasy. Thus, in this command, he wanted Timothy to continue fighting right beside him.[8]

This effort is "the good fight" (*ton kalon agōna*) in that it is what God expects His children to do. Since the gospel is truth, it is good to proclaim it and to stand up for it. The term "fight" is translated elsewhere as "conflict" (Phil. 1:30; Col. 2:1), "contention" (I Thess. 2:2), and "race" (Heb. 12:1).

D. Lay Hold (6:12b)

1. Nature of the command

The imperative "lay hold" (*epilabou*) is used of physical seizure, grasping, or contact: by Christ when He "caught" Peter as he began to sink into the waters of Galilee (Matt. 14:31), by Christ when He "took" the blind man by the hand and led him out of Bethsaida (Mark 8:23), by Barnabas when he "took" the converted Saul to the apostles (Acts 9:27), and by the slave masters who "caught" Paul and Silas at Philippi (Acts 16:19). In a metaphysical sense, it is used of the critics who tried to "take hold" of Christ's words (Luke 20:20) and of Christ who "took" on Himself the full human nature at His incarnation (Heb. 2:16). The latter use denotes full participation and appropriation. Paul thus charged Timothy to appropriate

8. The verb is a present middle imperative, deponent.

completely all that which God has graciously provided in redemption. The emphasis is upon present enjoyment, not upon that which takes place after death. The imperative could be paraphrased as "get a grip on."[9] Christ came to give both life and the abundant life (John 10:10). These can be enjoyed today when a believer obediently lives in the will of God.

The object literally reads "the eternal life" (*tēs aiōniou zōēs*). Eternal life begins at conversion, not at death or at the introduction of the eternal state (John 5:24). It is the very life of God in which a believer can share from the moment of his regeneration. To have Christ is to have life (John 14:6; I John 5:12). The emphasis is on the spiritual quality of life, not on its timeless duration, although it does encompass the latter.

2. Reasons for the command

The connective "whereunto" (*eis hēn*) literally reads "into which." The relative pronoun points back to its antecedent, "eternal life." The next two verbs explain why Timothy should appropriate eternal life.

First, Timothy was "called" (*eklēthēs*) by God into salvation. This is the efficacious call that manifests the divine purpose in election and issues in a justified position before God (Rom. 8:28–30). In the second epistle, Paul reminded Timothy of the power of God "who hath saved us, and called us with an holy calling, not according to our works, but according to his own purpose and grace, which was given us in Christ Jesus before the world began" (II Tim. 1:9). All believing sinners are divinely called (I Cor. 1:2). Paul also knew that he was a called apostle (I Cor. 1:1).

Second, Timothy "professed" (*hōmologēsas*) salvation. This verb shows his human response to the divine initiative. The calling is God's part in the redemptive program; the professing is man's part. Both are necessary in the provision and reception of eternal life. This confession probably occurred at the time of personal salvation (Rom. 10:9–10),[10] although some scholars have placed it at his baptism[11] or ordination.

9. Ingressive aorist middle imperative, deponent.

10. Homer A. Kent, Jr., *The Pastoral Epistles* (Chicago: Moody, 1979), p. 201.

11. A. T. Robertson, *Word Pictures in the New Testament* (Nashville: Broadman, 1931), vol. 4, p. 594.

Timothy's profession was "good" (*kalēn*) because it exalted God, exhibited an understanding of man's sinfulness and Christ's redemptive death and resurrection, and blessed the lives of those who witnessed it.

Timothy's profession occurred "before many witnesses." These witnesses knew that Timothy was saved and they could testify to the biblical accuracy and personal effectiveness of his profession.

II. THE CHARGE TO GODLINESS (6:13–16)

The rapport between Paul and Timothy is apparent in this section. The opening words contain the same verb employed earlier (*paraggellō;* 1:3; 4:11; 5:7). It also will be used later (6:17).

A. Witnesses to the Charge (6:13)

Believers had witnessed Timothy's confession of faith, but only the triune God could testify to his genuine obedience to the apostolic directive. Paul thus gave his charge "in the sight of" (*enōpion*) two divine persons.

1. God the Father

God is described as the one "who quickeneth all things" (*tou zōopoiountos ta panta*).[12] To quicken is to make alive. Divine quickening is necessary for both spiritual salvation (John 6:63; II Cor. 3:6; Gal. 3:21) and physical resurrection (John 5:21; Rom. 4:17; 8:11; I Cor. 15:22). Christ Himself was quickened by the Spirit at His resurrection (I Peter 3:18). God, who innately is self-sufficient life, can impart life. He did this in the natural creation, and He does it through redemption.

2. Christ Jesus

Christ is described as the one "who before Pontius Pilate witnessed a good confession." The phrase literally reads, "the good

12. The critical text has "the one who preserveth all things" (*zōiogonountos*).

confession" (*tēn kalēn homologian*), the same phrase used about Timothy (6:12). The historical allusion is to the trial of Christ before Pilate in the judgment hall at Jerusalem (Matt. 27:2, 11-26; Mark 15:1-15; Luke 23:1-26; John 18:28—19:16). Actually, Jesus appeared before Pilate twice, with a brief investigation by Herod Antipas occurring between the two trials before the Roman governor (Luke 23:6-12). In the face of false accusations hurled at him by the religious leaders, Christ responded to the interrogation of Pilate with divine composure and truth. When questioned about His kingship, He said, "Thou sayest that I am a king. To this end was I born, and for this cause came I unto the world, that I should bear witness unto the truth. Every one that is of the truth heareth my voice" (John 18:37). He thus declared and defended the truth of God's redemptive purpose even though He knew that He would be delivered to be crucified. He is subsequently identified as "the faithful and true witness" (Rev. 1:5; 3:14).

The direct result of Christ's confession was His crucifixion, but God quickened Him from the dead. The significance for Timothy was that God is in control of both life and death. Timothy knew that if he would be martyred for his confession, he had the full assurance that God would raise him from the dead. After all, Christ has "abolished death, and hath brought life and immortality to light through the gospel" (II Tim. 1:10).

B. Purpose of the Charge (6:14)

The purpose of the charge (6:14) is indicated by the English connective "that." It is actually an infinitive of purpose.

1. Description of the charge (6:14a)

The charge was "to keep the commandment" (*tērēsai se tēn entolēn*). In order to keep the commandment, a person must know what the commandment is, obey it, and teach it to others (cf. Rev. 1:3). The object ("the commandment") refers to all that Paul charged as a corporate oneness. Timothy was obligated to obey all of God's Word, but this term probably refers to the specific instructions of this epistle.

2. Attitude toward the charge (6:14b)

It was not enough for Timothy to keep the commandment. He also had to do this in the right way. Two means are given. The first deals with his attitude, whereas the second views his action. The first sees him as he is, but the second beholds him as he does. The first looks at the divine evaluation of his life, whereas the second stresses the human scrutiny of his ministry.

First, Timothy must keep the commandment "without spot" (*aspilon*). Christ was morally spotless (I Peter 1:19). Believers likewise have a responsibility to be separate from sin (James 1:27; II Peter 3:14). In the future, Christ will present the church, "not having spot, or wrinkle" (Eph. 5:27). The tongue, controlled by sin, is capable of defiling or spotting the entire body (James 3:6). The apostates themselves were moral spots within local churches (II Peter 2:13; Jude 12).

Second, Timothy must also be "unrebukeable" (*anepilēpton*). Paul used this word earlier to describe the "blameless" lives of pastors (3:2) and a characteristic of widows (5:7). As such, Timothy could prove to be a role model for other men in the gospel ministry.

3. Deviation from the charge (6:14c)

Timothy was instructed to keep the charge "until the appearing of our Lord Jesus Christ." The mention of Christ's return rather than the death of Timothy reveals the apostolic expectation that the Savior could have returned during their lifetimes.

The term "appearing" (*epiphaneias*) is derived from a verb that means "to shine upon" (*phainō* and *epi*). Its transliterated form is the English word *epiphany*. Both the noun and the verb are used to describe the first advent of Christ: His incarnation, ministry, death, and resurrection (II Tim. 1:10; Titus 2:11; 3:4). The term usually refers to the second advent, either to His coming for believers (II Tim. 4:1, 8; Titus 2:13) or to His destruction of the man of sin at Armageddon (II Thess. 2:8).

C. Basis of the Charge (6:15–16)

The relative pronoun "which" (*hēn*) refers back to its antecedent "appearing."[13] The time of Christ's appearing is known only to

13. Both are feminine singular.

God. It had not been revealed to Paul, but "in his times He shall show." This verb (*deixei*) is later used throughout the Book of Revelation for the divine disclosure of future events (Rev. 1:1; 4:1; 17:1; 21:9–10; 22:1, 6, 8). In His incarnate state, Christ did not know in His human consciousness the exact time of His return (Mark 13:32). In His humiliation, He chose not to exercise His divine attribute of omniscience. However, within the divine purpose for His postresurrection life, the Father has revealed the events that will precede Christ's return to the earth. John thus began the final book of the New Testament: "The Revelation of Jesus Christ, which God gave unto him, to shew unto his servants things which must shortly come to pass" (Rev. 1:1).

The basis of the charge is found within the purposes of the sovereign God of the universe. Since God controls the events of time, which will ultimately end in Christ's appearing, Timothy had to recognize that he would eventually be accountable to Him for the obedience to the Pauline charge.

Paul then presented a lengthy description of God. Although some scholars have tried to identify these verses with either the Father or the Son, it is better to see them as attributes of the one triune God who is Father, Son, and Holy Spirit.

1. God is the potentate

Three features are here. First, God is the "Potentate" (*dunastēs*). This term is applied to human governmental officials. In her magnificat, Mary declared that God had put down "the mighty" (Luke 1:52; same word). The Ethiopian eunuch, who was saved through the witness of Philip, was a man "of great authority" (Acts 8:27; same word). This noun is based upon a verb (*dunamai*) that means "to be able." A potentate, therefore, must have both the ability and the power to rule.

Second, God is "blessed" (*makarios;* cf. 1:11). Both He and His sphere of authority are marked by happiness and prosperity. Since He is blessed, He can impart His blessedness to those who meet the spiritual qualifications of His reign. The Beatitudes all begin with this same word (Matt. 5:3–11).

Third, God is the "only" potentate. All human and angelic

authorities are nothing when compared with God. They actually derive their influence from Him. By His very essence, God is absolutely exclusive. Only He could say, "Is there a God beside me? yea, there is no God; I know not any" (Isa. 44:8).

2. God is the King of kings

The phrase literally reads, "the king [*basileus*] of the ones who rule as kings" (*tōn basileuontōn*).[14] The title assigned to Christ is slightly different (*basileus basileōn;* Rev. 17:14; 19:16). God Himself removes and sets up kings within the movement of history (Dan. 2:21). All governments are actually ordained by Him (Rom. 13:1). All kings therefore derive their authority from His sovereign control and permission and are ultimately accountable to Him.

3. God is the Lord of lords

This phrase literally reads, "Lord of the ones who lord" (*kurios tōn kurieuontōn*). Again, the title assigned to Christ is slightly different (*kurios kuriōn*). In government hierarchy, lords are lower than kings. Another possible distinction is that the "lords" receive their authority from birthright whereas "kings" attain theirs by appointment or conquest.

4. God is immortal

God "only hath immortality" (*ho monos echōn athanasian*). This term literally means "no death." Immortality is an essential, underived divine attribute. God is self-existent; He has life in Himself (John 5:26). Paul earlier described God as "immortal" (*aphthartōi;* 1:17), but that term was a different Greek word meaning "without corruption." Human beings, who are subject to mortality or death, will become immortal when they receive new bodies through resurrection or translation (I Cor. 15:53–54). It is impossible for God to die. The only reason that Christ could die was because He gained a human nature through which He could experience the separation of His eternal self from the material body.

14. The first Greek term is a noun, whereas the second is an articular present participle.

5. God dwells in the light

God's eternal habitation is the light (*phōs oikōn*). God Himself "is light, and in him is no darkness at all" (I John 1:5). He is morally transparent. He is personified holiness. The psalmist claimed that God covered Himself "with light as with a garment" (Ps. 104:2). The eternal city has no need of light because God will be its light (Rev. 21:23–24; 22:5).

As light, God is totally unapproachable. The phrase ("which no man can approach unto") is the translation of one Greek term (*aprosition*).[15] It is a compound word meaning "not" (*a*), "toward" (*pros*), and "to go" (*ienai*). The brightness of His eternal, glorious being prevents all creatures, both human and angelic, from drawing near to Him. There is a moral, transcendant gulf between God and His creation.

6. God is invisible

Two statements about God's invisibility are given. First, He is the one "whom no man hath seen." This general statement covered all past history from Adam to Paul. The phrase "no man" literally reads "no one of men" (*oudeis anthrōpōn*). John categorically affirmed that "no man hath seen God at any time" (John 1:18). No man has ever looked upon the triune God in His eternal, spiritual omnipresence. When men saw God in ancient times (Gen. 32:30; Exod. 33:18–23), they actually saw a localized manifestation of God. They beheld Him as He appeared, not as He is.

Second, God is the one whom no one "can see." This general statement deals with the future, including both time and the eternal state. In the holy city, men shall see the face of God (Rev. 22:4), but again, they will view the manifested presence of God. In fact, it is most likely that men will see God only in the person of Jesus Christ, who is the visible revealer of God (John 1:18).

7. God deserves honor and glory

Paul ended this description of the qualities of God with a doxology: ". . . to whom be honour and power everlasting. Amen."

15. Used only here in the New Testament.

All believers should acknowledge verbally to God what He is by essence. He is the most precious person in the universe and He is the most powerful.

Questions for Discussion

1. What positive virtues should mark the man of God in today's world?
2. How can believers become more righteous? more faithful? more loving? more patient? more meek?
3. How can Christians fight for the truth? What is involved in compromise?
4. Why do believers fail to appropriate the full provisions of eternal life? How can this be overcome?
5. How can we Christians improve our witness to the lost? What are the qualities of a good confession?
6. What does the sovereignty of God mean to you? to your church? to your family?
7. Do believers have a good understanding of the basic nature of God? Do they know Him? If not, why not?

13

The Problems of Wealth and Intellectualism

I Timothy 6:17–21

The epistle ends with two final commands to Timothy: "charge" (6:17) and "keep" (6:20). The first pertains to his ministry to the rich believers, whereas the second constitutes a warning about the maintenance of doctrinal integrity.

I. THE CHARGE TO THE RICH (6:17–19)

The opening verse of this section actually begins, "To the rich in the now age give a charge. . . ." The emphasis is on the recipients of the admonition. These are rich, in contrast to those who desire to become rich (6:9). These are also rich believers in contrast to the rich unsaved. Although the possession of wealth has often made a person self-sufficient and less responsive to the gospel invitation (Matt. 19:23–24; I Cor. 1:26), some rich sinners have become Christians. Christ died for all, both rich and poor, and He seeks to save all lost men. He is no respecter of persons. Some believers, of course, have become wealthy after their conversion. Many men of wealth have also been godly: Abraham (Gen. 13:2), David, Solomon, other righteous kings of Judah, and Joseph of Arimathea, who placed the body of Jesus in his own tomb (Matt. 27:57). In the first century, it was virtually impossible for a poor man to become rich. These wealthy Christians, therefore, must have inherited their riches.

The phrase "in the now age" (*en tōi nun aiōni*) stresses the present situation in contrast to the future. In the eternal state, there will be no economic, racial, and sexual distinctions. Although the rich and the poor are positionally one in Christ, there is still a practical difference in their financial strength.

The command denotes a constant repetition of the charge (*paraggelle*).[1] This is the fifth and final use of this word (see also 1:3; 4:11; 5:7; 6:13). From this command issues a series of purpose infinitives that shows the goals of the charge.

A. Prohibitions (6:17a)

Two prohibitions are stated. The first views the opinion of the rich concerning themselves in relation to others, whereas the second points to their evaluation of their material possessions. The first looks at self; the second looks at things.

1. Pride

Timothy was to charge wealthy Christians to "be not highminded" (*mē hupsēlophronein*). Pride can become the curse of the rich. They can think that they are innately better than others simply because they have more. Riches normally produce security, power, and influence. A rich man can easily interpret this positional authority over others as personal superiority. Paul warned every believer "not to think of himself more highly than he ought to think; but to think soberly, according as God hath dealt to every man the measure of faith" (Rom. 12:3). In fact, he warned the Gentiles who had taken the place of the Jews within the redemptive program in the church, "Be not highminded [same word], but fear" (Rom. 11:20).

The possession of wealth per se is not an indication of divine favor. Moses cautioned, "But thou shalt remember the LORD thy God: for it is he that giveth thee power to get wealth" (Deut. 8:18). A person has received by the grace of God whatever abilities or wealth he may possess.

2. Trust in money

The second prohibition was not to "trust in uncertain riches." The verb (*ēlpikenai*) means "to set one's hope upon something or

1. Present active imperative.
2. Perfect active infinitive.

someone and to leave it there."[2] The proud wealthy have unfounded hope.

The value of hope rests upon the innate strength of the one on whom it is placed. Rich men's folly was to put hope upon things. They literally set their hope "upon the uncertainty of riches" (*epi ploutou adēlotēti*).[3] The irony is that they put hope on uncertainty, not even upon the riches themselves. The uncertainty is caused by the brevity of life (James 4:13–17) and the relative value of money, which is affected by inflation, war, and other complicated factors. Solomon warned, "He that trusteth in his riches shall fall" (Prov. 11:28). Jesus used the parable of the rich fool (Luke 12:16–21) to illustrate the folly of this false security.

B. Positive Goals (6:17b–19)

The strong adversative conjunction "but" (*alla*) marks the abrupt change from negative ends to positive pursuits.

1. To trust in God (6:17b)

The proper object of rich men's hope is described in three ways. First, they should set their hope "in the God" (*en tōi theōi*). They should trust in God, not upon gold.[4]

Second, rich men should trust "in the living one" (*tōi zōnti*). Hope must be in a living person, not in inanimate possessions.

Third, God is the one "who giveth us richly all things to enjoy." He is the rich provider of all that man needs. There is no limit to His infinite, gracious generosity. Moses refused "to enjoy [*apolausin;* same word] the pleasures of sin for a season; Esteeming the reproach of Christ greater riches than the treasures in Egypt" (Heb. 11:25–26).

2. To do good (6:18a)

The phrase literally reads "to work that which is good" (*agatho-ergein*). A rich man should put his money to work on that which

3. Used only here in the New Testament. However, see its use as an adverb (I Cor. 9:26).

4. Note the difference in the two prepositions: "in" (*en*) and "upon" (*epi*). The critical text, however, uses *epi* in both cases.

corresponds to God's innate moral goodness. Wealth must be seen as a divine stewardship and an opportunity to advance the kingdom of God. Believers are "created in Christ Jesus unto good works, which God hath before ordained that [they] should walk in them" (Eph. 2:10). One of those good works is to use money wisely and spiritually.

3. To be rich in good works (6:18b)

A believer who is materially rich may be poor "in good works" (*en ergois kalois*). Conversely, a Christian who is poor economically may be a spiritual plutocrat. The church at Smyrna, marked by deep poverty, nevertheless was rich before God (Rev. 2:9), but the Laodicean congregation was spiritually bankrupt even though it was affluent (Rev. 3:17). The Macedonians were praised for "the riches of their liberality" (II Cor. 8:2). A rich man is both foolish and poor when he lays up "treasure for himself, and is not rich toward God" (Luke 12:21).

4. To distribute (6:18c)

Rich men should be "ready to distribute" (*eumetadotous einai*). This phrase literally reads, "to be persons who impart their possessions in a pleasing fashion." The adjective is a compound word consisting of "well" (*eu*), "from" or "with" (*meta*), and "to give" (*didōmi*). Elsewhere Paul cautioned, "He that giveth, let him do it with simplicity" (Rom. 12:8). He also charged each believer to work "the thing which is good, that he may have to give to him that needeth" (Eph. 4:28). In order to give well, a believer must give willingly, bountifully, and purposefully (II Cor. 8:11–12; 9:6–7). He must give "not grudgingly, or of necessity: for God loveth a cheerful giver" (II Cor. 9:7). He must give joyfully and out of loving concern for those who are less fortunate than he.

5. To communicate (6:18d)

Rich men must also be "willing to communicate" (*koionōnikous*). This single word stresses joint sharing, having things in common. It is related to the word for "fellowship" (*koinōnia*). The emphasis is on financial sharing or communication. Paul so described the monetary support of preachers: "Let him that is taught in the word communicate [*koinōneitō*] unto him that teacheth in all good things" (Gal. 6:6). He praised the Thessalonians for their willingness to communicate with his needs through their financial gifts (*sugkoinōnēsantes;* Phil. 4:14–16). The rich believers should also fellowship financially with their poor spiritual brothers, especially the slaves (6:1–2).

6. To lay up treasure in heaven (6:19a)

The participle "laying up in store" (*apothēsaurizontas*) stresses the accumulation of treasure. This will automatically take place if the first five positive goals are realized. The paradox of benevolence is that the more one gives away the more he deposits in heaven. In the Sermon on the Mount, Jesus Christ declared,

> Lay not up for yourselves treasures upon earth, where moth and rust doth corrupt, and where thieves break through and steal: But lay up for yourselves treasures in heaven, where neither moth nor rust doth corrupt, and where thieves do not break through nor steal: For where your treasure is, there will your heart be also. (Matt. 6:19–21)

Solomon declared that "the liberal soul shall be made fat" (Prov. 11:25). He also stated, "There is that scattereth, and yet increaseth; and there is that withholdeth more than is meet, but it tendeth to poverty" (Prov. 11:24). The Scriptures constantly affirm that what is sown or given, not that which is stored for one's private use (II Cor. 9:6), is multiplied by God.

Through this financial generosity, a rich believer can lay a "good foundation against the time to come." The future reward for holy service, which is received at the judgment seat and subsequently enjoyed in the kingdom, is based upon present activity, including the stewardship of finances.

7. To appropriate life (6:19b)

When a believer lives for eternity, he better enjoys the reality of eternal life in the present. He recognizes the continuity between the two realms of personal existence. When the rich lay up treasure in heaven through liberal giving, they are able to "lay hold on eternal life."[5] Paul earlier charged Timothy to appropriate the real meaning of eternal life through a godly life and witness (6:12).

II. THE PROTECTION OF TIMOTHY (6:20–21a)

The direct address ("O Timothy") contains the only mention of the associate's name since the first chapter (1:2, 18). The exclamatory particle ("O") stresses the apostle's sense of urgency.

A. The Charge to Obedience (6:20a)

1. The command

The command "keep" (*phulaxon*) stresses vigilant protection, like that exercised by a military sentry or a prison guard (Acts 12:4; 28:16). The verb was used of the shepherds who kept watch over their flocks (Luke 2:8). In this epistle, it was earlier translated as "observe" (5:21).

2. The object

The object of the keeping was "that which is committed to thy trust." These seven words translate two Greek terms (*tēn parakatathēkēn*).[6] This compound word literally means "that which is placed down beside." It is a banking term, meaning "deposits." God had spiritually placed beside Timothy a sacred deposit of responsible leadership. His job was to defend the truth and to multiply its dividends. In the second epistle, Paul again charged, "That good thing which was committed unto thee keep [*parakatathēkēn phulaxon*] by the Holy Ghost which dwelleth in us" (II Tim. 1:14; cf. 1:12). One means of guarding truth is to disciple others who will likewise protect and propagate it in their generation. Paul thus charged, "And the things that thou hast heard of me among many

5. The critical text has "life indeed" (*tēs ontōs zōēs*).
6. The critical text has *parathēkēn*.

witnesses, the same commit [*parathou*] thou to faithful men who shall be able to teach others also" (II Tim. 2:2).

B. The Obstacles to Obedience (6:20b–21a)

Obedience involves "avoiding" (*ektrepomenos*) distractions that take a person's attention away from his main tasks. The verb, used earlier (1:6; 5:15), means "to turn away from." Timothy was to avoid two errors.

1. Babblings

The first problem was "profane vain babblings" (*tas bebēlous kenophōnias*).[7] The noun ("vain babblings") literally means "empty sounds or voices." These babblings have no doctrinal content. They make no positive contribution to spiritual development. The adjective ("profane"), used earlier (1:9; 4:7), stresses that such discussions are secular and worthless for genuine moral progress. In the second epistle, Paul gave the same charge: "But shun profane and vain babblings: for they will increase unto more ungodliness" (II Tim. 2:16).

2. Oppositions

The English term *antithesis* is the transliteration of the Greek word translated as "oppositions" (*antitheseis*).[8] The word literally means "to place against." This problem, therefore, centered in debate with a theological position that was diametrically opposed to biblical truth. In the context of the epistle, the opposition came from legalism, which is the archenemy of the gospel of the grace of God (1:7). Endless disputations with heretics invariably are counterproductive.

These oppositions have their origin in a "science falsely so called." The noun "science" (*gnōseōs*) can properly be translated as "knowledge" or "wisdom." The noun transliterates as "gnosis," the basis for the concept of Gnosticism. There is no reference here to the systems of laboratory science (e.g., biology).

7. Note that the conjunction "and" is in italics in the KJV.
8. Used only here in the New Testament.

Such knowledge is "falsely so called" (*pseudōnumou*).[9] It literally has a "false name," because it is not really knowledge at all. Knowledge presupposes the apprehension of truth, whereas this opposition was marked by commitment to error.

The relative pronoun "which (*hēn*) refers back to its antecedent "knowledge" (or "science").[10] Some teachers, in "professing" (*epaggellomenoi*) this falsely named system of knowledge, have actually "erred concerning the faith." The verb "erred" (*ēstochēsan*) was translated earlier as "swerved" (1:6). In the second epistle, Paul claimed that Hymenaeus and Philetus "erred" (same word) when they taught that the resurrection had already happened (II Tim. 2:18).

This error is concerning "the faith" (*tēn pistin*), the doctrinal fundamentals of redemptive truth. It does not refer to personal faithfulness, although a private faith in a system of error is naturally involved.

III. BENEDICTION (6:21b)

This benediction is one of the shortest within the epistles of Paul (cf. Col. 4:18; II Tim. 4:22). The apostle, to whom "the dispensation of the grace of God" was given (Eph. 3:2), desired that daily sustaining grace might be with his young associate.[11] God replaces grace with more grace in the lives of His children (John 1:16). His grace, which secured redemption through Jesus Christ (John 1:17; Titus 2:11), goes from eternity to eternity.

Questions for Discussion

1. Who is rich? How much money must one have in order to be known as a rich man? How does this standard vary in different cultures and generations?

2. Are many believers rich? Can a Christian become rich through divine goodness without committing the sin of selfish desire? How?

9. The term *pseudonym* is a transliteration of this word.
10. Both are feminine singular.
11. The critical text has the plural "you" (*humōn*) rather than the singular (*sou*).

3. In what ways are riches uncertain? Give illustrations.

4. In what ways can the rich manifest pride? How can they show humility in the midst of wealth?

5. What things does God give to all people for their enjoyment? Can money buy happiness? the opportunity for happiness?

6. How can the wealthy share their riches with the needy through the life of the church? How much money should they give to the work of the Lord? what percentage of their income? What provisions should they make for dispensing their estates?

7. Should a wealthy Christian leave money to unsaved relatives? Defend your answer.

Selected Bibliography

Bernard, J. H. *The Pastoral Epistles.* Thornapple Commentary series. Grand Rapids: Baker, 1980.

Guthrie, Donald. *The Pastoral Epistles.* Tyndale Bible Commentary. Grand Rapids: Eerdmans, 1972.

Hendriksen, William. *Thessalonians, Timothy and Titus.* New Testament Commentary. Grand Rapids: Baker, 1979.

Hiebert, D. Edmond. *First Timothy.* Chicago: Moody, 1957.

Kelly, J. N. D. *The Pastoral Epistles.* New York: Harper & Row, 1964.

Kent, Homer A., Jr. *The Pastoral Epistles.* Chicago: Moody, 1979.

Robertson, A. T. *Word Pictures in the New Testament.* Vol. 4. Nashville: Broadman, 1931.

Simpson, E. K. *The Pastoral Epistles.* Grand Rapids: Eerdmans, 1954.

Wiersbe, Warren W. *Be Faithful.* Wheaton, IL: Victor Books, 1981.

Wuest, Kenneth S. *Word Studies in the Greek New Testament,* vol. 12, *The Pastoral Epistles.* Grand Rapids: Eerdmans, 1952.